YOUR FRIENDS
THE TIBETAN REFUGEES

YOUR FRIENDS
THE TIBETAN REFUGEES

A CHRONICLE OF THE
TIBETAN AID PROJECT
1969–2000

Your Friends
The Tibetan Refugees

A Chronicle of the Tibetan Aid Project 1969–2000

The Tibetan Aid Project is an operation of the Tibetan Nyingma Relief Foundation Tax I.D. #23-743-3901. All contributions are tax-deductible.

The Tibetan Aid Project wishes to thank everyone who contributed to the production of this book. All proceeds from its sale will be used to preserve the Tibetan heritage for the benefit of future generations.

Photographic credits: photos on pp. 6, 16, 160 courtesy of Mary King; photo on p. 13 Joseph F. Rock © National Geographic Society, by permission; photos on pp. 18-35, 54 courtesy of Marilyn Silverstone/Magnum Photo Agency; back cover photo courtesy of Barbara Hirsch. All other photographs are from the archives of the Tibetan Aid Project and/or the Tibetan Nyingma Meditation Center, and are used by permission.

Published by Dharma Publishing on behalf of the Tibetan Aid Project. Typeset in New Aster and Caslon Openface. Printed and bound in the United States of America by Dharma Press.

ISBN No. 089800-325-3.
Library of Congress Control Number: 2001095840

9 8 7 6 5 4 3 2 1

Dedicated to the students of the
Tibetan Nyingma Meditation Center,
the staff and volunteers
of the Tibetan Aid Project,
and all who support the efforts of Tibetans
to transmit their cultural heritage

CONTENTS

TO TAP'S DONORS

IN APPRECIATION

Over the past thirty years, thousands of you have responded to TAP's appeals on behalf of the Tibetan refugees. Your donations of time or money demonstrate that you value the rich cultural and religious heritage of Tibet. Your interest and generosity have let TAP offer humanitarian assistance and implement projects that nourish the spirit of the Tibetan people.

TO THE PENFRIENDS You were the first to care. Your personal support for individual refugees saved lives, and your concern strengthened the Tibetan people as they adjusted to a radically different world. During the refugees' most difficult years, your letters and contributions helped thousands navigate the unfamiliar currents of the unknown seas into which they had been cast.

TO SPONSORS OF MONKS AND NUNS Your contributions will help the knowledge traditions of Tibet continue to benefit future generations. Your kindness has encouraged Tibetan centers to broaden their educational, artistic, and religious programs. Such generosity will come back to us all in the form of knowledge that can heal the wounds of conflict, offering inner peace.

TO OUR GENERAL DONORS You are the foundation of all TAP's projects and the engine that has sustained TAP's efforts for three decades. Coming from individuals in all walks of life, your donations demonstrate a wish to help a devastated people regain their culture, their dignity, and their ability to contribute their special qualities to the societies of our world. Added together, your contributions provide most of TAP's funding.

TO OUR LARGER DONORS Your support has allowed us to initiate important projects such as the shipment of sacred books to India and Nepal and the ongoing sponsorship of ceremonies. We are deeply grateful that you have seen the value of TAP's mission and have been inspired to support it.

TO EVERYONE As TAP's focus has shifted from survival assistance to cultural preservation, you have continued to give. While much work remains, you can take pride in what your generosity has accomplished. Tibetan children fed and educated with TAP's support in the 1970s are now leaders in the Tibetan exile communities. With their fellow Tibetans, they continue to rebuild their monasteries and nunneries, uphold their traditional values, and offer their priceless knowledge and the beauty of their culture to the rest of the world. Thank you for your years of loyal and continuing support.

PUBLISHER'S PREFACE

Tibet, a country of superb natural beauty and splendor, traces its civilization back more than two thousand years. The great king Srongtsen Gampo, who introduced Buddhism to the Land of Snow fourteen hundred years ago, was thirty-third in an unbroken royal succession. Five generations later, Guru Padmasambhava, Bodhisattva Shantarakshita, and King Trisong Detsen made possible a complete transmission of the Buddha's teachings. At that time Tibet controlled a vast empire, perhaps the largest of its era. Through succeeding generations, the Tibetan people maintained their independence. Proud and noble, yet humble in their spiritual lives, they were able guardians of the Buddha's legacy.

What truly set Tibet apart was its spiritual heritage. Songtsen Gampo, a manifestation of the Great Bodhisattva Avalokiteshvara, prepared the way for the blessings of Buddhism. He mandated the creation of a written language for translation of the Buddhist teachings and instituted a system of laws shaped by the principles of compassion and wisdom. Trisong Detsen and the great masters who worked with him built on this foundation to secure the Dharma for the Tibetan people.

For twelve centuries, Tibet benefited from this legacy. From nobles of the royal families to monks and yogins and nomads grazing their herds on vast plateaus, Tibetans lived in a world suffused with spiritual riches.

All this came to an abrupt end four decades ago. Tibet was occupied by a power hostile to its traditions and lost its independence. As the great monasteries, temples, and libraries came under attack, Tibetans streamed across the mountains into exile in India, Bhutan, and Nepal. Within a few short years, the light of the Dharma had grown dim in the land at the roof of the world, its healing rays obscured by dark clouds of hatred and intense suffering.

For those of us who escaped into freedom, the first years in exile were difficult beyond description. The people of India generously established emergency camps, provided essential care, and set aside land in remote regions for settlements, while H.H. the Dalai Lama provided compassionate leadership. Yet we had to cope with radical changes in customs, diet, and environment, the spread of serious diseases unknown in our native land, and the shock of having lost everything. Many did not survive the physical and emotional stress. Many more sank into apathy or despair. Yet others were able to use this terrible situation to deepen their realization of the truth of the Buddha's teachings. Twenty-five centuries ago, the Buddha Shakya-muni taught that actions based on ignorance, aggression, and selfishness inevitably produce suffering. Now we could see the truth of his words acted out on a grand scale. The evidence lay in the devastated lives of tens of thousands of Tibetan refugees.

As we tried to keep our bearings in the chaos and confusion of a world turned upside down, none of us knew what the next day would bring. At first the question we all asked was when we would be able to return home. No one could say, for the fate of Tibet was veiled in secrecy. It took months and even years before reliable news of our native land reached us in India. When it did, we learned the true horror of what our families and friends were going through. Tibet's new rulers were systematically dismantling our culture: razing the monasteries and educational institutions, destroying the books and art, and forcibly "re-educating" its long-suffering people.

From what we heard, our fellow Tibetans simply could not cope with this attack on their values, beliefs, and traditions. Many had lost their will to live. Others, driven half-crazy, were accepting the attitudes being drilled into them and joining in the destruction of their own culture. Never had Tibet faced such dark times.

Those of us in exile had limited resources, but the grim and saddening news we heard confirmed that we had a duty to act. If the Tibet in which we had been raised was becoming nothing more than a memory; if our people were losing their religion and culture along with their freedom, it was up to us to preserve what we had learned from our dear teachers and our families. We might not know what to do, but we had our memories and a little education, and no one was preventing us from acting. If we yielded to our sorrow or turned inward, the wisdom of the past might disappear from the face of the earth. But if we took heart and did all we could, there was still a chance that Tibetan civilization could survive to benefit future generations.

These reflections—which grew more urgent with each passing year—were close to my heart when I came to America in 1968. Soon after founding the Tibetan Nyingma Meditation Center (TNMC), I established the Tibetan Aid Project (TAP). Its aim was to make more widely known the plight of Tibetan refugees and to give Westerners a way to help the Tibetan people maintain their culture and values.

This book is a record of TAP's efforts and achievements in the three decades since its founding. Perhaps it can also serve as a lens through which to view the situation of Tibetans today, and as a reminder that the many accomplishments of the past four decades remain fragile. Tibetan culture is still at risk.

TAP's first operation was a simple exchange of letters and funds. Several TNMC students began to send ten or fifteen dollars a month to lamas and monks, receiving letters in return. For Tibetans in exile, such sums made it possible to study and practice, and let them dare for the first time to make plans for the future.

These early exchanges evolved into the Pen Friend Program. During its two decades of operation, more than 2,500 Western Pen Friends participated. Some became more deeply involved in the Tibetan cause, traveling to visit the refugees and offering their services.

Gradually TAP expanded its scope of activity, offering whatever support it could to the Tibetan refugee community. Following traditions established over centuries, TAP sponsored religious ceremonies at monasteries of all four schools of Tibetan Buddhism, so that the monastic way of life could continue in exile. It helped host visits of accomplished lamas of all schools to the West, and contributed to building monasteries and educational institutions in exile. Later, TAP collected money for the maintenance and improvement of the Maratika Caves in Nepal, Taksang Monastery in Bhutan, and other sacred sites. It also made donations to monasteries in Nepal, Sikkim, and Bhutan, lands where the Tibetan Dharma tradition had not been disrupted.

In the 1980s, I was able to visit my native land of Golok in East Tibet on three occasions. TAP joined TNMC in pledging funds for the reconstruction of Tarthang Monastery. This support made it possible to rebuild the chapel, the school of philosophical studies, and the temple, one of the largest constructed in Tibet since the occupation. After my visit to central Tibet in 1993, TAP began to support projects there as well. In all, TAP and TNMC have contributed funds to support the work of at least twenty monasteries, nunneries, and religious sites in central and east Tibet, and have offered modest funding on a regular basis to more than twenty monastic institutions in India, Nepal, and Bhutan.

In 1989, TNMC sponsored the first World Peace Ceremony in Bodh Gaya, India. It now takes place annually, with thousands of lamas, monks, and nuns in attendance. Over the years, we have produced and distributed hundreds of thousands and texts and art reproductions to the participants, an accomplishment made possible only through the time and energy of my students. Although most of the funding for the Ceremonies and for the production of texts and art has come from TNMC, TAP has played a key role, taking full responsibility for shipping the books and art that our organizations prepare for distribution each year. Twice TAP has organized pilgrimages in conjunction with the World Peace Ceremony, and the pilgrims have helped with the demanding task of distributing the texts and art to ceremony participants.

Throughout its existence, TAP's activities have been carried out by TNMC students and volunteers, none of whom receive compensation for their work. By keeping overhead to a minimum and avoiding waste, TAP has been able to ensure that all donations went directly to the organizations and individuals for whom they were meant. Even as costs have risen in recent years, TAP has done its best to maintain this policy. TAP also benefits from support by other Nyingma organizations. For example, Dharma Publishing has produced two previous books related to TAP's mission: *Ancient Tibet*, which introduces the study of Tibet and its early civilization, and *From the Roof of the World*, an account of the Tibetan community in exile.

In the years following Tibet's occupation, the fate of Tibet seemed shrouded in mystery. The world knew only that this once independent land had come under foreign control. With access impossible, there was no one to bear witness to the terrible suffering of the Tibetan people.

Today, the cause of Tibet and the contributions of Tibetan culture to world civilization are better known. Tourists travel regularly to a few places within Tibet designated for this purpose by the authorities, and international organizations monitor events there. Yet the horrors experienced by the Tibetan people over two decades remain poorly documented and understood. Perhaps one day light will be shed where there is now darkness, revealing the truth of what happened in Tibet and illuminating the more comprehensive truth of suffering on a vast scale. For now, we can offer our prayers, our candles, and our incense, asking for blessings for the unfortunate victims of such injustices, and for those equally unfortunate individuals who carried them out, whether willingly or unwillingly. The World Peace Ceremonies were founded in part for this purpose.

As for those of us still in exile, much has changed since the early years. We are much more in touch with the rest of the world. Many Tibetans have received advanced educations in countries on four continents, and are taking up professions and occupations that qualify them to participate fully in the modern world. Yet despite this progress, the situation of the Tibetan people remains precarious. Some things have not changed at all. Even those of us who live in fortunate circumstances no longer have a country to call our own. Hunger gnaws at us from within, for we are cut off from our culture, our traditions, and our sacred places. As individuals, more and more of us are free to take our place in the world community. But as a people, we are not free to choose our own way of life.

Buddhism teaches that situations arise through the workings of cause and effect. The tragedy of the Tibetan people, like all forms of suffering, must have its root causes in hatred, ignorance, greed, and selfishness. The Bodhisattvas know that all beings in the six realms suffer in their own ways, and viewed in this light we have no grounds for resentment.

Although we may not always maintain this way of looking, we have no choice but to absorb our sorrow. Lacking the power to alter our circumstances, knowing that violence and hatred never lead to good results, we must wait patiently for the healing light of truth to dawn. In our lifetimes, freedom of religion may yet return to our motherland. We may find ourselves celebrating a return to our own country, our own identity, culture, and language. If that day comes, I hope we prove ourselves worthy of it.

In terms of personal character and collective history, Tibetans display the same human weaknesses as any other people. They are fond of simple amusements and distracted by money, possessions, power, and intellectual interests. Yet as individuals, Tibetans manifest a dignity, warmth, and innocent goodness that others have often noted with admiration. Perhaps we can thank the majesty of our native land, the heritage of wisdom and compassion we enjoyed for so long, or our continuing heartfelt connection to the teachings of the Lord Buddha. Whatever the reason, most Tibetans seem to experience an inner peace that gives meaning to their lives. In my travels in many parts of the world since leaving Tibet, I have realized how rare this quality is, and have learned to appreciate the simple virtues of goodness and vitality that set Tibetans apart.

In today's world, however, change is accelerating out of control, and we can no longer take our national character for granted. As modernity fosters ways of thinking that call the survival of humanity itself into question, the old virtues may not be sufficient. The younger generation of Tibetans in exile have few defenses against the forces of change. Those raised as refugees readily get caught up in worldly concerns, while those who have only recently left Tibet, unable to imagine what it was

like to be in the first generation of refugees, are easily disappointed when their high expectations are not immediately met.

For this reason, the generation of leaders to which I belong has a special responsibility. Steeped in the ways of the past and educated in the tradition of Dharma, we have the resources to take decisive action. Fortunately, we have among us outstanding masters who demonstrate what a life devoted to Dharma can mean. One such master, renowned for his wisdom and compassion, was Chokyab Rinpoche. When he passed away recently, witnesses say that rainbows appeared in a clear sky: a traditional symbol of spiritual attainment.

From time to time in the course of history, aggression and ignorance generate enormous suffering on a scale so vast that the whole human race must take notice. To some extent, this is what has happened with Tibet. Perhaps, then, something positive can come of our people's sorrow: an increase in understanding that teaches humanity how not to repeat this kind of tragedy.

The story of the Tibetan people's suffering, and of their response to their national tragedy, holds lessons for people everywhere. Above all, however, it holds a lesson for the Tibetan people themselves. As we pursue our destiny, individually, culturally, and religiously, we cannot afford to forget our own past.

Whatever else can be said about the fate of our people, it remains true that in the end we have survived. In quiet, hidden ways, the traditions continue, despite all efforts at indoctrination into foreign systems of belief. Beyond the borders of Tibet, and beyond the communities of refugees, Tibetan culture has gained new recognition. The voices of many teachers, and especially the voice of H.H. the Dalai Lama, are heard clearly and honored in all parts of the world. Through the efforts of such masters, people in all lands have access to the Tibetan heritage in ways that would have been unthinkable fifty years ago. In these sense, a new chapter of Tibetan history is unfolding around us, based on the unique contributions the people of Tibet can make to the human quest for peace, understanding, and happiness.

However the destiny of the Tibetan people unfolds, the Tibetan Aid Project has a contribution to make. Its story is a story for the Tibetan people, but it is also a story of the kindness and generosity of thousands of Westerners. You have given financially when giving was not always easy. You have donated your time and energy when other demands called out insistently. Your steady efforts through all these years create unimaginable benefits, for in working for the people and the culture of Tibet, you are supporting the continuation of the enlightened lineage: humanity's great and enduring hope.

To the merits that your actions have already generated, I can only add my gratitude. On behalf of the Tibetan people and the Tibetan Aid Project, I thank you a hundred times over. Your kindness means a great deal to all of us. We will not forget.

Your Friends
The Tibetan Refugees

A CHRONICLE OF THE TIBETAN AID PROJECT

1969–2000

INTRODUCTION

THREE DECADES OF DEVOTION TO A CAUSE

The lama Tarthang Tulku arrived in Berkeley, California in 1969. Trained in the Tibetan Buddhist tradition by many of the greatest lamas of the twentieth century, he had been forced into exile in 1959 as a result of the occupation of Tibet by a foreign power. Now the traditions of his native land were under siege. It was up to the Tibetans living as refugees in India, Nepal, and other parts of the Himalayas to assure that the knowledge preserved in Tibet for twelve centuries was not lost to the world.

Although he had few resources, Tarthang Tulku was intent on preserving Tibet's heritage of wisdom and compassion. Soon after his arrival in Berkeley, he founded the Tibetan Nyingma Meditation Center and began offering teachings on Buddhism to Westerners. As his students learned of the desperate conditions faced by Tibetan refugees, they joined in the relief efforts that Tarthang Tulku initiated. They gathered clothing and shoes to send to India and contributed small sums of money out of their own resources. These early activities marked the beginning of the Tibetan Aid Project (TAP). Staffed entirely by volunteers, TAP was formally incorporated in 1974.

Three decades after its founding, TAP's mission to preserve the cultural heritage of Tibet remains essentially unchanged. Tibetan culture, so greatly weakened from the loss of its homeland and many of its leading masters, today must cope as well with the increasing impact of Western-style influences that affects all of Asia. TAP has responded by supporting monastic institutions and individual practitioners, working year round to raise funds that go to all traditions of Tibetan Buddhism. At the same time, it works to increase awareness and appreciation for Tibetan culture in the West.

Those of us who have given our best efforts to TAP over the years view our work as a precious opportunity to preserve for humanity one of its greatest resources. This book grows out of our love and respect for Tibet's cultural and religious traditions. In gratitude for what we have learned, and out of the wish to benefit our own culture, we offer this account of TAP and the people and culture it serves.

PART ONE

THE TIBETAN PEOPLE IN EXILE

CHAPTER ONE

A GREAT CIVILIZATION
AT THE ROOF OF THE WORLD

The Tibetan plateau is a natural wonder. Protected by towering mountain ranges held sacred by the people of many lands, its glaciers are the source of all the major rivers of Asia. Nowhere else do people live at such high elevations, so close to wind and sun, stars and sky. For the rest of the world, Tibet has long been a land of mystery, a hidden Shangri-la where profound and miraculous visions can emerge from the mist.

Legend has it that the Tibetans are descended from a marriage between a Bodhisattva monkey and a female ogre. The ogre belonged to one of the twelve tribes of non-humans who ruled Tibet in succession after a great lake formed by melting snows had drained away, making the land habitable. The monkey was a manifestation of Avalokiteshvara, the Bodhisattva of Compassion, long revered by the people of Tibet as their special protector.

After the era of the non-humans, Tibet is said to have been peopled by a number of tribes, each its own small kingdom. The first king to unite these principalities and create a sovereign Tibet was Nyatri Tsenpo, who was most likely born in 247 B.C.E., the time when Ashoka was consolidating a great empire in India.

The royal succession established by Nyatri Tsenpo continued for forty generations. From the Yarlung River valley, the domain of the early rulers, the kingdom gradually extended its borders throughout the central provinces. In the seventh century C.E, under the Dharma king Srongtsen Gampo, Tibet expanded beyond the plateau to become one of the world's great empires, incorporating most of Central Asia and extending its reach into China and India. Even after the empire collapsed some two centuries later, Tibetan culture continued to influence vast regions of Asia down through the centuries.

Largely undiscovered in the Age of Discovery, virtually unaffected by the Industrial Revolution that spread from Europe and North America throughout the world in the nineteenth and twentieth centuries, Tibet continued to maintain a sophisticated culture. Explorers and travelers told of a great civilization concealed in the Himalayas, but for

Opposite: Sacred architecture ornaments the natural splendor and power of the Tibetan landscape.

Westerners such accounts must have seemed half-legendary.

For the few foreigners who did enter the Land of Snows, Tibet presented a seeming paradox. On the material level, its people lived the simple, timeless lives of nomads and farmers. The land was sparsely populated, and travel was so difficult that a journey from east Tibet to the capital city of Lhasa could take many months. Yet here and there on the journey one would find buildings whose imposing facades, like that of the famed Potala Palace in Lhasa, more than matched the architecture of other lands. Those who visited the great monasteries found refined works of art, elaborate religious festivals, and carefully maintained libraries: signs of sophisticated creativity, high purpose, and inspired knowledge.

Those who remained longer discovered a still greater paradox. Wrapped in its splendid isolation and mountain beauty, Tibet preserved the unbroken lineage of teachings that could be found in their entirety nowhere else in the world. Here in this isolated land, the Tibetan people maintained as a vital living presence the teachings of wisdom and compassion given to the world by the Buddha Shakyamuni, who lived and taught on the plains of India more than 2,500 years ago.

BUDDHISM IN TIBET

Well before the Classic Age of Greece laid the foundation for civilization in the West, Prince Siddharta Gautama was born in the kingdom of the Shakyas, in the border lands between India and Nepal. Through dedication, resolve, and penetrating insight, Prince Siddhartha became the Buddha Shakyamuni, master of perfect enlightenment. Through his teachings and through the Sangha of monks, nuns, and lay people that formed around him, the Buddha revealed a way of life based on wisdom and compassion and shaped by a path of inquiry and openness. Through his own example and the knowledge he passed on, the Enlightened One offered all beings freedom from sorrow.

The teachings of the Buddha spread throughout India and the rest of Asia, nurturing a living tradition of wisdom and compassion. Through oral instruction and in thousands of texts and commentaries, great masters of the Dharma explored every field of knowledge, from philosophy, religion, and ethics to logic, art, history, and medicine. In the eighth century C.E., when this transmission was in full flower, the Dharma flowed like a great river into the valleys of Tibet.

THE DHARMA ENTERS THE LAND OF SNOW

Symbols and texts of the Dharma first reached Tibet in the fourth century, during the reign of Lha Tho Tho Ri, the twenty-eighth king of Tibet. Three centuries later, Srongtsen Gampo, thirty-third in the royal lineage, united the Tibetan people and forged a strong empire. Determined to prepare his kingdom for transmission of the Dharma, he sent his minister Tonmi Sambhota abroad (to either India or Kashmir) to develop a script and language suitable for translating Buddhist texts. The king entered into marriage alliances with the Buddhist lands of China and Nepal and enacted a new constitution based on Dharma principles. To subdue Tibet's wild natural forces and prepare the land to receive the transmission of the living Dharma lineage, he built temples in outlying areas of his kingdom.

Five generations later, in the middle of the eighth century, King Trisong Detsen initiated the full transmission of the Dharma to Tibet. Second of the three great Dharma kings, he invited Shantarakshita, abbot of the famous university of Nalanda in northern India and the greatest pandita of his time. Shantarakshita initiated construction of Samye, Tibet's first monastery, but obstacles arose. The abbot advised the king to invite Padmasambhava, the Guru from the northwestern land of Oddiyana. Padmasambhava quickly pacified the hostile forces obstructing the foundation of the teachings and gained their support. In fulfillment of an ancient prophecy, Abbot, Teacher, and King created the conditions for Tibet to become a land of Dharma.

When Samye was completed, the king invited 108 panditas to Tibet to work with Tibetan translators trained in the Dharma. In little more than a generation these teams translated thousands of texts. Among the great panditas was Vimalamitra, foremost scholar of Oddiyana. Chief among the Tibetan translators was Vairotsana, master of many languages, disciple of the greatest gurus of all Dharma lands, and accomplished teacher in his own right.

In the ninth century, the third great Dharma king, Ralpachen, won fame for his unwavering devotion and support for the monastic Sangha. Ralpachen established a commission that reviewed the translation work done earlier and regularized the language used for giving expression to the Dharma. After his untimely death, Tibet endured several generations of disruption and disorder. During these dark times, the teachings were preserved in secret in the central provinces, as well as by masters who sought refuge in eastern Tibet.

When order was restored in the tenth century, Buddhism once again became the guiding force in Tibetan culture. Although some Tibetans continued to follow the pre-Buddhist religion of Bon, the vast majority practiced the Dharma, naturally cultivating a harmonious and balanced way of life.

A SECOND DHARMA TRANSMISSION

Late in the tenth century, a second wave of Dharma transmission began, bringing new Tantras, commentaries, lineages, and systems of practice to Tibet. From the seeds planted during this transmission arose schools known as the Sarmapa, or New Tradition schools. Those who continued the original lineages transmitted to Tibet in the eighth and ninth centuries now became known as Nyingmapa, followers of the Ancient Tradition.

From the eleventh century onward, monasteries were built in all parts of Tibet. The Land of Snows became a living mandala, rich in monuments to the Dharma, full of temples, sacred art, and precious texts. Great teachers in the Nyingma and Sarma schools preserved and transmitted the living lineage of the teachings through study and practice, and the Tibetan people benefited from a way of life in which devotion to the Dharma illuminated each activity and every concern.

THE MAJOR SCHOOLS

NYINGMA SCHOOL

The Nyingma tradition preserves the lineages brought to Tibet during the early propagation of the Dharma. For more than twelve centuries, great masters have upheld its special teachings, known as Kama and Terma. In the fourteenth century, the incomparable Longchenpa systematized these two streams of teachings and created a foundation for all future Nyingma studies. In the seventeenth century, Orgyen Terdag Lingpa and his brother Lochen Dharmashri, the founders of Mindroling Monastery, revitalized the tradition, and in the eighteenth century, the all-knowing Jigme Lingpa compiled the Kama teachings and continued the lineage of realization that Longchenpa had established, helping to systematize its practice. In the nineteenth century, Jamgon Kongtrul, working together with the famed masters Jamyang Khyentse and Chogyur Dechen Lingpa, collected and compiled the Terma teachings into the Rinchen Terzod. Later that century Lama Mipham systematized the Nyingma philosophical view, writing works that made important contributions to all areas of learning and practice.

Although the Nyingma tradition has never relied on a strong central organization, prominent masters established or expanded six major monasteries during the seventeenth and eighteenth centuries to perpetuate the transmission of the Kama and Terma lineages: Kathog, Dorje Drag, Mindroling, Payul, Dzogchen, and Zhechen. Branch monasteries established in other parts of Tibet also became major centers for Dharma study. Some exceeded their mother monasteries in size and in the number of monks and lamas.

At different times and in different places, the Nyingma tradition has emphasized yogic practice, meditation, or scholarship as the situation required. Its great masters included Tertons and yogins famed for their power to work magic and produce wonders. While each of the major Sarma schools held temporal authority at various times, the Nyingma tradition never sought political involvement. It focused more on the lives of the common people than on maintaining large institutions.

KADAM SCHOOL

The origin of the Sarma schools is closely linked with Lord Atisha Dipamkara Shrijnana (982–1054), the famed master from Vikramashila University in India. At Vajrasana Monastery in Bodh Gaya Atisha won the respect of all Buddhist traditions for his perfect conduct, and at Vikramashila he became India's leading pandita.

Invited to western Tibet by Lha Lama Yeshe Od, a ruler who had joined the monastic order, Atisha labored tirelessly to restore the Sangha in Tibet. At Toling Monastery, he worked with the great scholar Rinchen Zangpo, at that time a very old man. On his way back to India, Atisha met Dromton Gyalway Jungnay, who had come in search of him. Moved by Dromston's devotion, Atisha agreed to stay in Tibet. Visiting Samye Monastery, the learned pandita was amazed to discover texts he had not seen even in the libraries of India's great universities.

Regarded as a manifestation of Padmasambhava, Atisha was not only a scholar, but a siddha, and Terma master as well. In Tibet, he revitalized the monastic Sangha on a strong moral basis, In the teachings he gave his disciples, he focused on how to follow the path to enlightenment by taking refuge, studying Mahayana philosophy, and putting the teachings into practice through following the Bodhisattva ideal.

After Atisha passed away, Dromton led his fellow disciples to Todlung, and in 1056 established Reting monastery. Later masters in this lineage included Tumton Lodro Dragpa, who founded Narthang Monastery in 1153, and Ngog Loden Sherab, the noted translator and scholar. From this nucleus arose the Kadam school. Following the lead of Atisha, the Kadampa emphasized direct transmission from master to disciple to ensure that the teachings would be accurately presented and passed down. Famed for the purity of their practice, they preferred to live as hermits and built few monasteries.

Lacking a strong central organization, the Kadampa did not survive as a formal school. Their lineages, however, were continued in all schools and by independent masters. Several centuries later, they became the basis for the Gelug school.

KAGYU SCHOOL

The lineages of the Kagyu tradition trace to the Indian Mahasiddha Naropa and his teacher Tilopa. Naropa became the teacher of Marpa Chokyi Lodro (1012–1097), a Tibetan who traveled to India three times to obtain teachings from the great siddhas and scholars. Marpa's disciple Milarepa (1040–1123), who held all of Marpa's teachings, helped establish the practice of meditation and devotion as central to the Kagyu tradition.

The main stream of Kagyu teachings flowed through Milarepa's disciple Gampopa, branching through Gampopa's disciples into four major and eight subsidiary traditions, including the Drug, Taklung, Karma, and Drigung: the four schools that are most prominent today. Another major division of the Kagyu tradition, the Shangpa Kagyu, traces to Khyungpo Naljor (978–1079), a powerful siddha and famed scholar who studied the Mantrayana systems in Nepal and India under great masters, yogins, and yoginis.

In later centuries, many of the Kagyu schools were actively involved in Tibetan politics, mostly through alliances with Mongol lords. The second Karmapa, Karma Pakshi, was invited to the courts of Kublai and Monge Khan in 1254, while the third and fourth Karmapa incarnations both spent time in China at the request of the last Mongolian emperor. The Tsalpa, the Drigung, and the Phagmo Dru schools all held power at one time or another.

SAKYA SCHOOL

The Sakya tradition was founded by Khon Konchog Gyalpo (1034–1102), a descendant of generations of Dharma masters. His master, Drogmi Shakya Yeshe (993–1050), had studied with the great masters of India. Drogmi transmitted to Khon Konchog Gyalpo and other disciples the teachings known as Lamdre, or teachings of Path and Fruit, made known by the siddha Virupa

In 1073, Khon Konchog Gyalpo founded the Sakya or Gray Earth Monastery. His work was continued by his son Sachen Kunga Nyingpo, the first of the Five Great Masters considered the founders of the Sakya tradition. His two sons, Sonam Tsemo and Dragpa Gyaltsen, were succeeded by their nephew, Kunga Gyaltsen (1182–1251), also known as Sakya Pandita: the supreme teacher of the Mongols and the greatest scholar of the Sakya school. His nephew Pakpa (1235–1280) also enjoyed the veneration of the Mongol court. As a direct result of this relationship, when the Mongols embarked on their conquest of China and Central Asia, they did not invade Tibet, placing it instead under the regency of the Sakya leaders. Pakpa's successors continued to wield political influence for another century.

The Sakya tradition has always emphasized scholarship. At Zhwalu Monastery, founded in Tsang in 1040 by the Sakya master Jetsun Sherab Jungne, the fourteenth-century scholar Buton reviewed thousands of Dharma texts and shaped them into the Tanjur and Kanjur, the Tibetan Buddhist canon. Lhundrub Teng Monastery in Derge in east Tibet, built in the fifteenth century by Tangton Gyalpo and famed for its printing house, was the site three centuries later for the preparation of the Derge edition of the Kanjur and Tanjur, widely considered the most authoritative of all editions.

Within this strong scholastic tradition two major subschools developed: the Ngor, founded by Ngorchen Kunga Zangpo (1382–1456), and the Tsar, founded by disciples of Tsarchen Losel Gyatso (1502–1566). A major artistic center, Ngor Monastery housed five hundred resident monks and large numbers of students. The center for the Tsarpa was Yarlung Tashi Chode Monastery, founded by Tsarchen's disciple Yolwo Zhonnu Lodro.

GELUG SCHOOL

The founder of the Gelugpa tradition, Je Tsongkhapa, was born in Amdo in east Tibet in 1357. Tsongkhapa studied first under the Kadam master Choje Dondrub Rinchen and received ordination from Karmapa Rolpay Dorje. An outstanding scholar, he traveled widely, collecting the Kadam lineages and studying the major Sarma Tantras under Sakya and Kagyu masters.

In 1410, Tsongkhapa founded the monastery of Ganden in central Tibet. Here he established the New Kadam school, also known as the Ganden and

Opposite: A monk at Cho-ne Monastery, with the wood blocks for the Tibetan Canon

eventually as the Gelug school. The new school drew heavily on the teachings of Atisha and on the extensive commentaries written by Tsongkhapa himself.

Known for his devotion to Vinaya practice, his knowledge of the Sutras and shastras, and his mastery of logic and debate, Tsongkhapa introduced monastic reforms and emphasized a strong monastic Sangha and central administration. The founding near Lhasa of Drepung and Sera monasteries gave the Gelug school a strong institutional basis. Accommodating between four and nine thousand monks each, both monasteries functioned as virtual cities. Tsongkhapa's many disciples soon extended the Gelug Sangha, founding 140 monasteries throughout Tibet. Riwo Gegya Ling Monastery in Mongolia eventually became the largest of all Gelug monasteries, with a resident population of 27,000 monks.

Tsongkhapa's three leading disciples were Gyaltsab Darma Rinchen (1364–1432), Khendrub Gelek Palzang, and Gendun Drub, posthumously recognized as the first Dalai Lama. In 1447, Gendun Drub built Tashi Lhunpo Monastery near Shigatse in western Tibet. In the sixteenth century, the Mongols bestowed the title of Dalai Lama on the young master Sonam Gyatso (considered the third in the lineage), and thereafter became patrons of the Gelugpa.

The incarnation lineage of the Panchen Lama was first recognized in the seventeenth century. Tashi Lhunpo, by then a large educational center housing four thousand monks, became the seat of the Panchen Lamas, and the lineage of Dalai Lamas transferred their seat to Lhasa's Potala Palace. The Fifth Dalai Lama, Ngawang Lozang Gyatso (1617–1682), respected by all Tibetans for his enlightened guidance, forged an alliance with the Mongols that established the succession of Dalai Lamas as temporal rulers over Tibet. The Fifth Dalai Lama's regent, the outstanding scholar Sangye Gyatso, made lasting contributions to Tibetan culture.

INTERPLAY AND INSPIRATION

Traditionally Tibetans recognized eight distinctive teaching lineages, which today have merged into the four major schools. The three activities of teaching, debating, and writing were honored in all schools as the "three excellent endeavors," for they contributed to the growth of the Dharma and disseminated its benefits. Pursuing these paths, the masters of all four schools created a rich and bountiful heritage of knowledge. Debates among the scholars of all schools refined the understanding of the profound doctrines presented by the Buddha and clarified by the great masters of India, Tibet, and other Buddhist lands.

At the most basic level, the Tibetan people revered the works produced by the great masters of all schools as priceless treasures. They viewed the heritage of inner realization and insight transmitted by these masters as the shining light of their civilization.

A TIMELESS CIVILIZATION

Tibet evolved a way of life that focused inward on spiritual transformation rather than outward toward material gain or worldly power. As the world beyond the Himalayas underwent a revolution in its way of life, Tibet's teachers, monks, and yogins kept Tibetan culture focused on the revolution in human understanding that the Buddha had initiated and brought to perfection. In each generation new leaders arose, masters whose penetrating awareness, meditative insight, and compassionate actions allowed them to transmit the heart of the Buddha's realization. Students in the great monastic schools, yogins who practiced on glaciers and in mountain caves, and village lamas who guided the daily affairs of the people all relied on a path grounded in profound insight and devotion to the welfare of others.

Monasteries served as the cultural and educational centers of Tibetan life. The larger monasteries housed extensive libraries with collections of sacred texts, some dating back over twelve hundred years. A few monasteries preserved the wooden blocks from which new copies of texts could be printed, and lamas often copied over manuscripts of rare texts. The temples were repositories of splendid works of sacred art: paintings, murals, bronze statues, and decorative elements with profound symbolic significance. Over six thousand monastic and religious centers dotted the land, serving as the cultural heart of each village, town, or region.

Tibetan families considered it an honor and an obligation to have at least one son or daughter enter monastic life, where the circumstances were best suited for the study and practice of the teachings of the Buddha. It has been estimated that one-quarter of the male population lived in monasteries as lamas, monks, and novices, while a smaller percentage of women became nuns. Monastic residents engaged in religious practice and carried out ceremonies. At the same time, they created remarkable works of sacred art and devoted themselves to study of philosophy, logic, grammar and literature, history, medicine, and other disciplines meant to serve the spiritual and practical needs of the people.

Guided by the sublime teachings of the Buddha, the people of Tibet had learned to live in harmony with the powerful natural forces of their mountain plateau. Largely undeveloped in a material sense, in all other respects theirs was one of the world's great civilizations. Its teachers pursued subtle forms of inner understanding with all the engaged sophistication of physicists at work on a far-reaching theory of the interplay between matter and energy. The light of the Buddha's teachings shone in every valley and each individual's heart. Transmitted in an unbroken lineage of insight, the teachings illuminated the acts and circumstances that make up each human life.

CHAPTER TWO

A DESPERATE SITUATION

In the mid-twentieth century, major changes that affected the whole of Asia began to disrupt Tibet's traditional way of life. In 1949, after decades of armed conflict, the Communist party took over China. Soon the new leaders began to implement their vision of a new society based on materialistic values and the totalitarian control of political and social institutions.

Committed to a view of history that regarded Tibet as a part of China, the new regime was determined to assert its claims over the Land of Snows. They also intended to put an end to what they regarded as Tibet's outmoded, superstitious, and backward way of life.

As detailed in a recent comprehensive history of this era by the scholar Tsering Shakya, Chinese leaders embarked on a complex series of political maneuverings and military actions that mixed threats and actual armed hostilities with promises of aid for modernization. Within a few years their army had taken over much of eastern Tibet. In central Tibet, the Chinese leaders adopted a policy of appeasement, while intruding ever more strongly into the affairs of government. In 1959, after nearly a decade of increasing encroachment, this uneasy coexistence gave way to full control. The Red Chinese army entered the capital city of Lhasa and proclaimed the "Autonomous Region of Tibet" to be a part of China.

As the threat posed by the Chinese army became unmistakable, H.H. the Fourteenth Dalai Lama, leader of the Tibetan state, fled into exile in India. Making the dangerous journey across the Himalayas on horse and on foot, he took up residence in Dharamsala, a former British Hill Station made available by the Indian government, and established a government in exile.

Soon thousands of Tibetans began to follow in their leader's footsteps, Despite grave risks, they undertook the journey through the treacherous mountain passes. Traveling largely by night to avoid the occupying army, many lost their lives in the desperate attempt to escape; others were captured along the way. Those who completed the journey safely arrived exhausted and in near despair, having lost almost everything they held most dear.

Opposite: the ruins of Dorje Drag Monastery in central Tibet, destroyed some time after 1959

Carrying all they owned, Tibetans arrived in India in shock from what had happened.

To block the mass exodus, the Chinese increased their border patrols, making the strenuous journey still more dangerous. Yet the stream of refugees continued for several years, until repression by the authorities grew so extreme that flight became almost impossible. Estimates of the number of refugees vary (for a discussion, see A. Tom Grunfeld, *The Making of Modern Tibet*) but most sources appear to agree that as many as a hundred thousand refugees attempted the journey; an official publication by the Office of the Dalai Lama in 1969 estimated the number who had arrived safely in India and Nepal at eighty-five thousand.

In 1966, China entered the era of the so-called "Cultural Revolution," which undertook to eradicate all manifestations of traditional culture. Cadres of Red Guards were dispatched to Tibet, where they set about destroying Tibet's religious centers, discrediting religious practitioners, and barring all forms of religious expression. During the next few years, monasteries that had stood for centuries were razed, their libraries and temples ransacked and desecrated. Carved wooden blocks that had been used to print sacred texts were taken to be used as railroad ties. By most accounts, all but thirteen of Tibet's 6,300 monasteries, together with their vast collections of Buddhist texts, sculptures and sacred paintings, were destroyed. (According to Grunfeld, the Chinese acknowledged only 2,500 monasteries, but admitted that all but ten had been destroyed.) For many years the Dharma could be practiced only in secret.

Starting in 1959, and especially during the dark years of the Cultural Revolution, the Tibetan people experienced

Dazed, hungry, and exhausted, they came on foot, by mule, and on horseback.

years of great hardship, marked by forced "re-education" and mass imprisonments, as well as famines brought on largely by the imposition of farming policies unsuited to Tibet's environment. According to the International Campaign for Tibet, which monitors conditions in Tibet, an estimated 1.2 million Tibetans—over one sixth of the ethnic Tibetan population—perished in these early years. While the threat of famine receded over time, attacks on Tibetan civilization intensified. In time even the use of Tibetan language in schools and official transactions was discouraged and in part prohibited.

Today Tibetans can practice the Dharma within narrow limits, but the damage to their traditions has been extensive. Except in a few remote regions, the teachings that made Tibet itself a land of profound spiritual beauty have all but vanished.

STARTING OVER

The refugees who made their way into India and Nepal were numb from their ordeal and disoriented by the immensity of their loss. At first they hoped that their situation was only temporary; that someone would take up their cause and expel the invaders. Rumors of military action circulated widely. H.H. the Dalai Lama sought to bring the plight of the Tibetan people to the attention of the United Nations, but the geopolitical situation was complex. Although the people and nations of the world expressed their shock and their sympathy for the Tibetan people, no one could find a way to translate such sentiments and concerns into effective action.

*The huts at an early refugee settlement: a place for the refugees to recover
their strength and face the reality of living in exile.*

*In the jumble of the camps, friends rediscovered each other and strangers, their accents
almost incomprehensible to one another, spoke of their shared fate.*

Refugees too exhausted to travel on foot the final leg of the journey to the refugee camps are transported by tractor and cart.

A famished horse forages in the barren fields where Tibetan refugees are spreading out their few remaining belongings.

After the ordeal of their harsh journey, a time to rest and attempt to make sense of what has happened.

No one had any any idea what the future held. Would it always be chaos and disorder, exhaustion and uncertainty?

In the rough democracy of the camps,
lamas and lay people mingled freely.

Accustomed only to barley, Tibetans
wondered if rice and dal were really edible.

The heat of the Indian plains was a shock for the refugees.
It drained what little energy they had left.

For the newly arrived, exhaustion warred with relief, uncertainty with sorrow.

Thinking back on what they had left behind; wondering about the future, the refugees had to look deep within for the resources to survive.

*Does anyone know what happened to my mother and father, my aunts and uncles,
my brothers? Has anyone seen the Rinpoche s from the monastery?*

A layman performs his daily prayers as Indian soldiers look on. Many refugees had left behind food and necessities in favor of sacred texts and ritual objects.

Although they were safe in the camps and could count on food and medical attention, the new arrivals did not know what the future held in store. Still, they could draw support from one another.

A first tentative step toward the future: an outdoor classroom to teach Tibetan to the children.

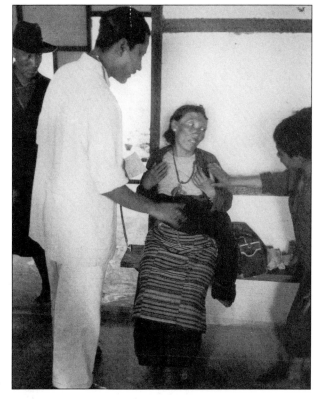

Diseases such as tuberculosis and dysentery spread rapidly in the crowded camps, and the risk of infection was high. Young children and the old were at special risk.

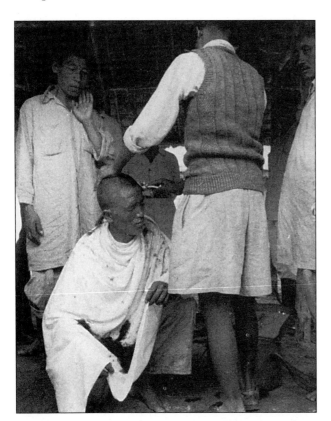

Old rituals and new influences mingle; past certainties face the unknown future.

Tibetans who had been processed through the transit camps were often sent out to work on road gangs. The work was difficult and dangerous.

The government in India, where most of the refugees fled, made great efforts to provide food and housing. Two major refugee camps were established. One proved unworkable, and was soon closed, but the other, at Missamari near Tezpur, would operate for the next ten years. Built in the spring of 1959, it consisted of large bamboo cabins that housed from thirty to forty refugees each, or more in times of acute need. With a maximum capacity of nine thousand, Missamari Transit Camp became a central way station for many of the refugees. The Indian authorities struggled to process the new arrivals quickly so that they could be sent on to other relocation centers when they had recovered from their journey. But often there was simply no place for them to go.

Life at Missamari, as documented in the pictures on the preceding pages, presented new arrivals with nearly overwhelming challenges. The environment was radically different from anything they had experienced before. Living conditions were crowded and unsanitary, and infectious diseases spread quickly. Perhaps more damaging, however, was the tremendous sense of loss experienced by every refugee. Not knowing if their loved ones were alive or dead, wholly ignorant of the fate of their beloved leaders, teachers, and monasteries, they faced an uncertain future, bereft of the cultural support and sense of purpose that give life meaning.

In those early days, most of the refugees felt that somehow their fervent prayers to be restored to their homeland would be answered. Few Tibetans had any real sense of the global politics at work, and many believed that since their cause was just, the nations of the world would support them. Only gradually did the weary and heartsick refugees realize that a foreign power was firmly in control of their native land and determined to maintain its rule. The nightmare in which they found themselves was real, and they had to do their best within the conditions it presented.

Tarthang Tulku has written of these difficult times:

In many of the refugee camps, tuberculosis was running rampant, and all around us friends and relatives were falling victim to disease. For those who avoided this danger, the overriding question was how to survive. The Indian government initiated a program that employed many refugees on road gangs. Traveling back and forth across India breaking up rocks along mountain highways for a few rupees a day, these individuals were able to provide for their daily necessities, but only at the cost of physical exhaustion that dulled the mind. Work was dangerous, with many fatalities.

Other refugees set up tea stalls or tried to find similar ways to make a living. Many had come from highly cultured backgrounds in Lhasa and elsewhere, and such individuals found it especially difficult to adjust. I remember seeing people whose minds had apparently cracked under the strain, sad figures who paced endlessly back and forth, talking to themselves. Others kept their sanity, but were broken in spirit. Hopeless, they simply sat and stared.

At the same time, some younger people seemed possessed by a kind of craziness, a sense that now that the old world was gone, they were free to do whatever they pleased. Their wild and shocking behavior —at least by all traditional standards—was yet another source of pain for their elders.

For the few hundred lamas who had managed to escape into exile, the tension was impossibly great. Deeply attuned to the depth of Tibetan culture, they recognized the danger that their whole civilization might simply vanish. Most found it difficult to imagine continuing their traditions when the monasteries and libraries were lost, the great holy places inaccessible, and the basic resources for study and practice suddenly gone. Tarthang Tulku has written:

At first the enormity of our loss overwhelmed any sense we might be able to continue on our own. True, we could go on with our studies, provided that the texts were available. We could preserve our language, and for at least a time, we could preserve our traditions. But what would happen over the course of the coming decades? How could a community of sixty or seventy thousand refugees, all impoverished, keep a whole culture intact?

Still, the situation was not entirely hopeless. The lamas had their education and training, and their years of study and meditative practice had taught them how to deal creatively with each new situation and turn obstacles into opportunities. Beyond that, they shared an unwavering dedication to working for the Dharma and for the welfare of other beings.

As the lamas took stock of their situation, they realized that vital parts of their heritage remained accessible, at least in scattered form. The thousands of refugees streaming across the high mountain passes had brought with them revered texts and sacred works of art, often choosing to carry these objects of spiritual value in place of the food and clothing that might have improved their chances of surviving the perilous journey. These precious treasures could be the foundation for new monasteries and schools, essential for training a new generation for the uncertain times ahead.

In any case, the lamas in exile realized that they had no choice. If Tibetan civilization was to survive this devastating blow, it would be through their ongoing commitment and efforts. The burden of transmitting the knowledge that flowed through its ancient traditions rested on their shoulders.

PART TWO

FOUNDING OF TAP: FOCUS ON FRIENDSHIP

CHAPTER THREE

STARTING OVER: INDIA AND AMERICA

Among the lamas who found themselves in exile in India was a young man named Tarthang Tulku. Born in Golok in east Tibet, in a region that the Chinese now declared to be a part of Qinghai Province, Tarthang Tulku belonged to the Nyingma school of Tibetan Buddhism. The son of a well-known lama who had left his monastery to live among the people, Tarthang Tulku was recognized at an early age as a tulku, or incarnation, and was taken to Tarthang Monastery for training. As a very young man, he received permission for a journey that would let him meet and study with the greatest masters of eastern Tibet. Over the next eight years, he traveled to different monasteries and retreat centers, receiving a comprehensive education in Buddhist teachings and related disciplines.

In 1958 Tarthang Tulku left Tibet to join Jamyang Khentse II, his root guru, in Bhutan. When the Chinese seized control of Tibet in 1959, he was already safely outside the country, engaged in an intensive retreat. As he has written:

I was one of the lucky ones. I had left my native Tibet to be with my beloved master Jamyang Khentse, so I did not have to flee under cover of darkness, nor did I have to dodge the bullets of my pursuers. Even in Bhutan I was deeply fortunate, for I had some silver and coins, as well as goods that I could sell to support myself. It was almost a year before my funds were exhausted.

Like his fellow Tibetans, Tarthang Tulku was now an exile, but at first this did not dramatically change his circumstances. When his teacher passed away late in 1959, he broke off his retreat to journey to Sikkim, where he paid his respects to his guru's remains. He then embarked on a lengthy pilgrimage to the Buddhist holy places of India. Next he journeyed to the Himalayas, where he meditated at the sacred sites of Rewalsar, Lahul, and Spiti. As time passed, however, the truth of his situation became painfully clear. Perhaps the youngest of all the lamas in exile to have received a comprehensive traditional education in Tibet, Tarthang Tulku knew that much depended on his efforts. He began to consider how he could best use his energy and training to be of benefit.

Opposite: "I am glad you all enjoyed my telling stories. You know, my dear children, even if poverty overtakes you, you can make yourself happy and that will make others happy too."

Left: Tarthang Tulku in 1959, shortly after leaving Tibet. Right: While serving as a visiting scholar at Sanskrit University, Tarthang Tulku meets with a learned Gelugpa lama.

As he was pondering a course of action, an unusual opportunity presented itself. Scholars of Buddhism in India had begun to realize that Tibet's misfortune had at least one benefit from their perspective: the arrival in their midst of highly trained scholars from a tradition of Buddhism with close historical ties to India's own culture. The faculty at Sanskrit University in Varanasi managed to obtain fellowships for four Tibetan lamas, one from each of the major schools, who would join the faculty and contribute to its work. When an older lama declined to serve as representative of the Nyingma school, H.H. Dudjom Rinpoche, who had been chosen head of the Nyingma school in exile, asked Tarthang Tulku to accept the fellowship. In 1962, Tarthang Tulku left the Young Lamas Home School in the hill station of Dalhousie, where he had been studying, and took up his new position on the faculty of Sanskrit University.

Once at the university, Tarthang Tulku found that his duties as a member of the faculty were modest. Apart from occasional lectures and meetings, conferences and tutorials, he could devote himself to study and to discussions with a few senior faculty and with his fellow lamas. Eager to do more, he determined to use his monthly stipend of five hundred rupees to found a press that would print and distribute vital texts he had brought with him from Tibet. He found a dilapidated garage that could be repaired to suit his needs, borrowed five thousand rupees to purchase a small hand press, and started operations. He named the new press Dharma Mudranalaya, in honor of the great printing house at Derge Monastery in east Tibet.

Living on nothing but rice and dal to save money, Tarthang Tulku was able to pay living expenses for a small staff of Tibetans, Indians, and Westerners out

Dharma Mudranalaya is a newly inaugurated press in the city of Benares devoted to the publication of those manuscripts which are infused with the light of Buddha's wisdom.

The sacred texts of the Nyingmapa and Kargyudpa living traditions are now in danger of becoming extinct. The transmission of these teachings at this time, to those who will read with an open heart, should be as a wish fulfilling gem which grants eternal happiness.

Tarthang Tulku, a Research Fellow of Sanskrit University, is the publisher who has during the past years been gathering together the people and materials for this task. A press has been acquired and representatives of the Kargyudpa and Nyingmapa sects have been invited to reside at its site.

Now there is some difficulty. Expenses are not finished and the press has not yet begun working.

With good fortune and your help many wonderful ideas could be realized. The press could become a center for study and scholarship. English and Hindi language translations, as well as the Tibetan texts, could be published, and the light of Dharma circulated around the world.

Address all correspondence c/o
Tarthang Tulku,
Dharma Mudranalaya
C. 21/1C, Maldaiya
Varanasi-2, (U. P.)
India.

of his stipend. None of the group knew anything about printing, so he trained himself in the necessary skills, even arranging for the calligraphy and casting of a Tibetan typeface. Despite numerous obstacles, over the next few years Dharma Mudranalaya was able to publish more than twenty Tibetan texts.

For the next several years, Tarthang Tulku focused on printing and publishing and on his scholarly and academic duties. He made contact with eminent Indian and Western scholars, and also came to know some of the young Westerners traveling through India in search of spiritual knowledge.

Circumstances shifted again in the late 1960s. A new institute for Tibetan studies was being founded in Sarnath, near Varanasi, and the original program under which Tarthang Tulku had been engaged came to an end. After considering various options, he decided that he could be most effective in serving the Dharma and working for Tibetan culture by traveling to the West. In 1968 he left India. After traveling in Europe, he arrived in the United States later that same year. In February of 1969 he came to the San Francisco Bay Area, where he soon settled in Berkeley, a vital and dynamic university town where people were awakening to Tibetan Buddhism and the potentially life-transforming effect of its teachings.

CREATING A LIVING MANDALA

As one of the first lamas to come to the West, Tarthang Tulku was committing himself to introducing Tibet's rich heritage of realization to a culture where most people had never even heard of Tibet. At the same time, he was dedicated to preserving and restoring the cultural and spiritual legacy of Tibet. Soon the vision he brought with him inspired a structure that could accomplish both aims.

As he explained to his students in later years, the structure that Tarthang Tulku gradually established in America was based on the mandala, a symbol of creativity and cosmic order. The principle of the mandala emphasizes the harmonious relationships of each part to the whole, and its forms evoke a sacred energy and dynamic with the power to lead beyond ordinary limits and concerns and overcome obstacles to success. Rinpoche (a title of respect used by his students and supporters) determined to apply the mandala principles in shaping the activities he intended to pursue in the West. During his first decade in America, he established the organizations that would give content to the mandala's structure.

At the center of the Nyingma mandala is the Head Lama of the Tibetan Nyingma Meditation Center. Operating under the direct authority of Tarthang Tulku as Head Lama, the Meditation Center, often referred to simply as TNMC, was established as a Corporation Sole in 1969, just months after Tarthang Tulku settled in California. The mission of TNMC is to preserve and transmit the symbols, sacred literature, teachings, and forms of Buddhism, with a special emphasis on the Tibetan Nyingma tradition. It provides both vision and spiritual guidance to the Nyingma organizations and to the

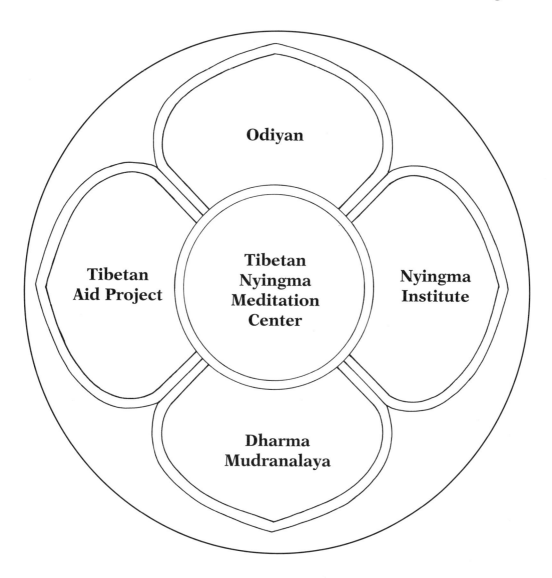

students who make up the Nyingma community. The activities of all the other Nyingma organizations express aspects of this guiding vision. The Odiyan Monastery and Country Center, founded in 1975, and the Yeshe De Project, officially formed in 1983, are projects so closely related to TNMC's goals that they have remained under the direct supervision of the Head Lama.

In the east (shown in Buddhist art in the lower quadrant of the mandala, the point of entry to its structures) stands Dharma Mudranalaya, successor to the printing house Tarthang Tulku founded in India. Formally incorporated in 1975, Dharma Mudranalaya is dedicated to printing and publishing translations of Buddhist texts and commentaries, traditional art, and other works that make the knowledge conveyed through the Tibetan traditions available to a Western audience. The east is associated with beginnings, and Dharma Mudranalaya has developed in harmony with this principle. Operating as Dharma Press (which

Tibetan Nyingmapa

Meditation Center

an introduction. . .

TIBETAN REFUGEE LAMAS

Tibetan refugee Lamas are of special concern to the Center. Since the unfortunate invasion of Tibet in 1959, over 4,000 Lamas have managed to escape to sanctuary in India where they subsist in minimum-sustenance circumstances. *It is important to realize that of all the ancient civilizations of the world, Tibet is the last to survive intact to the present day.* For this reason it is especially vital that this generation of Lamas in India be allowed to continue their researches. On this premise the Center collects and forwards used clothing, or any helpful commodity; and each student is responsible for one Lama's support (eight dollars a month), providing the bare necessities. Still, many Lamas remain in gravest need. The Center provides names and addresses to all who wish to aid and correspond with the refugee Lamas.

MEMBERSHIP

Membership in the Center is divided between Practicing Students and General Membership. Practicing Students, directly trained by the Rinpoche, are selected by personal interview. Once accepted, the student is expected to meet a monthly pledge of fifteen dollars, a sum selected as reasonable by the existing students.

Members are divided into several classes:

1. Friends of the Tibetan Center participate in its work by pledging ten dollars monthly.
2. General Members pledge ten dollars yearly.
3. Donors forward a gift of one to five-hundred dollars.
4. Sponsors give from five hundred to one thousand dollars.
5. Lifetime Members pledge one thousand dollars.

It is also possible to directly sponsor scholarships for outstanding young Lamas in universities in India.

Excerpts from one of the earliest TNMC brochures, published just a few months after Tarthang Tulku settled in Berkeley. It included an appeal for support of refugee lamas.

prints texts and art) and Dharma Publishing (which distributes them), it has introduced hundreds of thousands of readers to the treasury of Buddhist teachings. It has produced the *Nyingma Edition of the Tibetan Buddhist Canon*, which gathers into 120 atlas-sized volumes the entire Tibetan Buddhist Canon. In addition, it has published over a hundred titles in English that explore the great depth and vast range of Buddhist teachings, and has joined with the Yeshe De Project to produce thousands of texts in Tibetan. Today Dharma Publishing is the largest Buddhist publisher in the world.

The Tibetan Aid Project is found in the south of the mandala, the direction associated with resources and foundation. Active since 1969, the Tibetan Aid Project (TAP) was incorporated in 1974. Originally focused on helping the community of Tibetan refugees to survive, TAP was gradually able to shift its efforts to supporting the preservation of Tibetan culture. Today, TAP supports the preservation projects of TNMC and helps educate the public about Tibetan culture and the Tibetan refugees. It funds the distribution of texts and art to Tibetans, sponsors ceremonies at monastic centers in India, Nepal and the Himalayan regions, and offers assistance to religious centers and individuals as they work to keep the spirit of Tibetan culture alive.

In the west of the mandala, associated with beauty, fruition, and communication, stands Odiyan, a monastery and retreat center created as a home for the Dharma in the West. Named for the birthplace of Padmasambhava, founder of Buddhism in Tibet, Odiyan is home to six major temples and the golden Enlightenment Stupa. Its architecture, art, prayer wheels, and prayer flags manifest the splendor of the teachings, and provide an appropriate setting for the Yeshe De Project's production work.

In the north of the mandala, associated with accomplishment, is the Tibetan Nyingma Institute, established in Berkeley in 1972. The Institute is the educational center of the Nyingma organizations. By offering classes, retreats and workshops, it presents the rich Buddhist heritage of Tibet to the public. The Institute also serves as a doorway to the rest of the Nyingma community. Many community members made their first connection through attending Institute programs.

Full-time members of the community donate their time to Dharma projects and activities, receiving only a small stipend to provide for their basic needs. Through participating in the structures of the mandala, Rinpoche's Western students have learned that their work offers an invaluable opportunity to cultivate the qualities of generosity, integrity, patience, vigor, concentration, and wisdom that form the foundation of the Bodhisattva path.

The work of each of the Nyingma organizations can only be fully understood within the context of the entire mandala structure. Often the various organizations share responsibility, each taking on different aspects of a project in order to achieve a common goal. Although the focus of the Tibetan Aid Project on the needs of Tibetans sets it apart from the other organizations, its successes have come through shared efforts that engage all parts of the mandala. Through the good fortune of having Rinpoche's continuing guidance, TAP has been able to balance its own mission with the activities of the community and achieve some measure of long-term accomplishment.

MAKING CONNECTIONS

By the time Tarthang Tulku arrived in the San Francisco Bay Area in 1969, almost ten years had passed since the occupation of Tibet. Caught up in the fervor of the Cultural Revolution, the authorities occupying Tibet were making a concerted effort to eliminate every trace of the Buddhist culture that had guided the Tibetan people for twelve centuries. Tibetan libraries and monasteries that had previously been left to decay or put to use as granaries were now being systematically destroyed, and the practice of religion was virtually prohibited. For the Tibetan people it was the worst of times, perhaps the darkest years of a nightmare that continues to this day.

In the camps and settlements of the refugee community, there were no restrictions on practice of the Dharma, and progress was being made toward self-sufficiency. Yet the struggle was long and difficult, and most of the Tibetan exiles did not yet enjoy the kind of economic stability that would let them think about the long-term goal of cultural preservation.

In Berkeley, Tarthang Tulku faced a different set of challenges. Americans had only a very limited understanding of Tibet, its Buddhist heritage, and the vast losses it had endured. Their knowledge of the situation for the refugees was even more sketchy. Most of the students in Rinpoche's classes were well-educated in Western terms, and they had a strong wish to learn more about meditation or Buddhist philosophy. But it was more difficult for them to comprehend the dangers and difficulties faced by the Tibetans in exile, or to understand fully why they should care about what happened to people who lived so far away and under such vastly different circumstances.

BEGINNINGS OF THE TIBETAN AID PROJECT

Gradually, Rinpoche began educating students in the importance of preserving what remained of Tibetan culture, encouraging them to offer help to the refugee community. Later, Rinpoche described these first small steps: "The sufferings of my lama friends were never far from my mind. My students joined in collecting clothing to send to the refugees in India and pledged small monthly donations to lamas in need as a way to assist the refugees and support their efforts to reestablish their culture." These early efforts marked the birth of the Tibetan Aid Project.

TAP's first major initiative was the Pen Friend Program (described in Chapter Four). TNMC students sent modest donations each month to individual refugees, along with letters inviting an exchange of correspondence. To augment this support, several students took on other projects typical for small organizations trying to raise funds. These included rummage sales, auctions, and stalls at craft fairs and flea markets. These events helped publicize the desperate conditions faced by the Tibetan refugees. At the same time, they gave Rinpoche's students a way to introduce the public to the newly established Nyingma organizations in their midst.

By now, Rinpoche's talks and classes were attracting leading thinkers, educators, health professionals, scholars, and religious leaders. Their support made it possible for TNMC and TAP to expand the scope of their activities on behalf of the refugees. The first of several art exhibitions organized by TNMC introduced the beauty and achievements of Tibetan civilization, conveying without words the values of wisdom and compassion underlying Tibetan culture.

In 1971, TNMC purchased an abandoned fraternity house not far from the campus of the University of California. Renamed "Padma Ling" (Lotus Ground), this grand old building, which predated the 1906 earthquake, would become TNMC's permanent home. For the first time, TNMC students could live in a community setting, pooling their resources and dedicating their full-time efforts to Dharma projects. A large room at Padma Ling known as the Project Office became headquarters for TAP, which continued to expand its activities. During these years Rinpoche was developing an approach to daily work that showed how the challenges of each new task could serve as a way to practice the Buddhist path. This approach to work, which became known as Skillful Means, proved both inspiring and effective. By applying its methods, TAP's staff soon found themselves taking on more ambitious projects than they had dreamed possible.

EARLY ACTIVITIES

Among TAP's early fundraising efforts were screenings of the best films available on Tibet and Tibetan Buddhism. These included *Requiem for a Faith*, a film that featured grainy black and white footage of Tibet in the days before the invasion. Several documentaries on the Tibetan diaspora, loaned to TAP by the Indian consulate in San Francisco, showed in graphic terms how desperate the situation was for Tibetan refugees.

In 1973, the opening of the Nyingma Institute (housed in another old fraternity house near the university campus) made it possible to invite the public for special events. The new building was soon offering an expanded array of well-attended classes. TAP hosted a series of small dinners accompanied by slide shows, a model for fundraising it would take up again twenty years later. The Institute also sponsored several seminars whose proceeds were dedicated to TAP's goals. With themes such as "The Interface between Eastern Meditation and Western Psychology" and "Science and Mysticism," these programs

hinted at the contributions Tibetan culture could make to the West.

TAP also sought support from Bay Area artists, literary figures, and musicians, who gave poetry readings and concerts. A series of benefit piano concerts at Stanford University drew enthusiastic crowds, happy to lend their support to a worthy cause.

A Presence in Nepal

Even after a decade in exile, the shortage of medical care remained a major concern for the refugees. Tuberculosis, cholera, dysentery, and hepatitis, aggravated by malnutrition, stress, and dehydration, were all common. Tibetans had no immunity to most of these diseases, which were unknown in Tibet, and traditional Tibetan doctors had no experience diagnosing or treating them.

In 1972, Rinpoche's wife Nazli went to Nepal on behalf of the Tibetan Aid Project. The plan was to set up a temporary medical clinic, while assessing what could be done to cope with the problem on a long-term basis. The clinic was established in Bodhnath, on the outskirts of Kathmandu, where many of the refugees had congregated. Although its resources were limited, it could offer antibiotics, skin ointments, multiple vitamins, first aid kits, and bandages. Clinic staff also distributed clothing and dehydrated food.

During the six months it operated, the Nepal clinic provided care to many individuals who had received little or no medical attention since their long journey from Tibet. Unfortunately, despite fundraising efforts in Nepal, resources

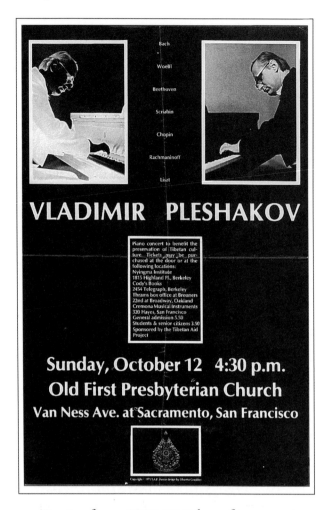

Poster for a 1975 TAP benefit concert

were not available to establish a professionally staffed clinic on a permanent basis. However, two of the doctors who had volunteered with TAP later traveled to India independently to treat an entire Tibetan village for a year.

During her stay in Nepal, Nazli bought some property in Bodhnath to house a permanent clinic. When it became clear that TAP did not have the staff or financial resources to mount such a major project, the land was placed in the care of Jampal Lodo, a Tibetan lama living in Nepal. Jampal Lodo later made it available to H.H. Dilgo Khyentse, who developed it years later as the site for his monastery,

Zhechen Dargye Ling, guided today by H.E. Zhechen Rabjam.

GIVING TAP A VOICE: GESAR NEWS

In 1973, TNMC began publishing *Gesar News*, which featured Dharma teachings along with information about the activities of TNMC and its related organizations. Many of Gesar's first readers were TAP supporters, eager to learn more about the status of the Tibetan refugees and the impact that their contributions were having. The first issue set the tone for later presentations with an article that focused on the refugee situation. Written by a TNMC student who had stayed with Khenpo Palden Sherab, a Tibetan lama in Sarnath, the article portrayed the efforts of the Nyingma community in Sarnath to build a monastery and library on land purchased with the help of TNMC and TAP. It concluded with a plea for help:

Tibetans have great difficulties as refugees. The Nyingma Center tries to help as much as possible by sending money to refugee camps and monasteries and coordinating the Pen Friend Program. Interested people can ask for the name of a Tibetan lama who needs help. The students at Sarnath have all requested pen friends, but not all have one as yet. For as little as ten dollars a month all the basic necessities can be purchased in India; more is a great help. Many warm friendships have arisen in the past four years between Tibetans and Americans.

We can also arrange support for refugee children, many of whom live

The first issue of Gesar

finished monasteries being built by the refugee communities, together with a plea for funds.

In 1974, *Gesar* reported that over a hundred thousand Tibetans were still living in refugee camps in India, Sikkim, Nepal, and Bhutan. In addition to enrolling hundreds of new participants in the Pen Friend Program, TAP at this time was actively seeking grants for direct aid. Both the Lily Endowment and the Irwin Sweeney Miller Foundation made one-time grants.

Despite some improvements in their living conditions, the refugees continued to struggle to obtain basic necessities. A first-person report in the Fall 1974 issue of *Gesar* offered a glimpse into the circumstances of their lives:

in orphanages because they have lost their families or their parents must work on roads or construction sites far away to survive. . . . To help, please contact the Center and we will give you the name of a Tibetan needing support and explain the best ways to send money.

By the end of its first year of publication, *Gesar* had evolved into a quarterly magazine. Over the next several years, almost every new issue carried a report about TAP and its activities, repeatedly pointing out that a small monthly donation could provide all the basic needs for a monk, a nun, or a small child. Many issues also carried photos of half-

My first stop was the Nyingma Lamas College in Dehra Dun, about 200 kilometers northeast of New Delhi. . . . I began finding out details about the Lama's College: its way of life, its means of support, its relationship to the Indian government, and the availability of food and medical supplies. The lamas could still buy enough food, but inflation was obviously hurting them since their money was marginal to begin with.

We walked out into the heat across a flat dirt field. An Indian army colonel has lent the college a bulldozer so the fields could be cleared for planting, and now they needed a well for irrigation. Unfortunately, the machinery might have to come from New Delhi. (I thought of my twelve-hour ride by bus from Delhi and tried to calculate in my mind the cost of bringing heavy equipment across miles of bad roads.) In front of us was a large, partially complete building, which will be a Tibetan temple with side rooms for a library, living quarters, and a medical dispensary.

Arrangement have been made for a doctor to visit once a week, but medical supplies and equipment will have to be brought and maintained by the college. Unfortunately, there is not enough money to finish the building. Even though much of the finish-work can be done by Tibetans and many of the thankas and statues for the temple are already available, the price of raw materials and Indian labor is going up all the time. Work on the building will soon have to stop if more money cannot be raised. Meanwhile the young lamas continue to live in rough "barracks" furnished only with tiered bunks, with no privacy at all for study and meditation.

. . . In Manali I made two visits to the mountain retreat and monastery of Khenpo Thubten Mewa. I showed him pictures of the Berkeley Institute from Gesar and talked with him about Tarthang Tulku and students in the United States. The conditions and hardships for the Khenpo and his students could not help but impress me. They had very poor quality food—almost no meat and not much fruit. Several of the students were at least mildly sick. They live in very small rooms, either in caves that have been dug out of the mountainside or in small cottages.

. . . It was also clear to me in Manali how dearly the Tibetan refugees are paying for their forced move from Tibet. One highly respected young lama of the Kagyud school (Apo Rinpoche) died while I was there. Some of his students had tried to find a local doctor willing to walk to their monastery to see him. They could not find one. The Tibetans in India are suffering from diseases they never contracted in Tibet. The hot climate, too, is radically different from the climate in Tibet, and the Tibetans, with their compact, muscular builds, their traditional heavy clothing and their rich "butter tea" are obviously aliens in the Indian landscape.

LEGAL INCORPORATION OF TAP

TAP had begun as an arm of the Tibetan Nyingma Meditation Center, the center founded by Tarthang Tulku in 1969. As its operations expanded, it continued to be closely linked to the Meditation Center, and its staff was actively involved in a variety of TNMC projects.

The success of the Pen Friend Program (see next chapter) gave TAP a specific function well suited to the early needs of the refugee community. It soon became clear, however, that TAP could be far more effective in dealing with the complex regulations controlling the transfer of funds to India if it had its own corporate identity and organizational structure. On November 8, 1974, the Tibetan Nyingma Relief Foundation (TNRF) was incorporated as a California non-profit public-benefit corporation, registration number 725771.

Lamas engaged in study and practice formed the backbone of refugee communities.
Young monks found time for play, while lay people worked to survive.

*Above: Armed with pick and shovel, carrying sand in bags and mixing concrete by hand,
Tibetan refugees in India work at building a new school for their community.
Below: Monks in exile beat roasted barley to make tsampa, the national food of Tibet.*

Soon after, TNRF received approval as a tax-exempt organization under Internal Revenue Code sections 501(c)(3) and 170(b)(1)(A)(ii) and California Revenue and Taxation Code 23701(d). The new entity was assigned Federal identification number 23-743-3901.

The decision to create a new corporate structure quickly proved its worth. TAP's ability to send funds to India and Nepal directly meant lower bank fees and helped overcome some of the difficulties that individuals had been experiencing in trying to send funds on their own. For the first time since its founding, TAP now had access to complete and accurate information about how much money was being sent and who was receiving it. For their part, donors who gave money directly to TAP could deduct the full amount of their contributions from their taxes.

SOUND BUSINESS ON DHARMA PRINCIPLES

Along with Rinpoche's other students, the staff of TAP actively practiced Skillful Means, making their work a part of their Dharma practice and using their Dharma studies to increase the effectiveness of their efforts. In addition, Rinpoche applied special rules for TAP. Above all, he insisted that donations received by TAP be used to the fullest extent possible for the purposes the donors intended.

To succeed at this goal, TAP adopted operating procedures that most other non-profits would have found impossible to maintain. None of the TAP staff received any compensation for his or her work, not even the modest stipend provided other full-time TNMC students to help cover living expenses; instead, stipends for TAP volunteers had to come from other sources. Strict rules also applied to administrative costs and overhead, which had to be kept to a minimum and paid for from sources other than donations. While some non-profits spend as much as seventy percent of their income on administrative costs, Rinpoche asked TAP to keep this amount to under five percent. Purchases of equipment or supplies beyond a bare minimum were strongly discouraged.

TAP operated under these guidelines from 1974 through 1993. During this time, 98% of donated funds went directly to program services in India and Nepal—a truly remarkable achievement matched by very few organizations. In later years, new policies were established to take into account the cost of increased mailings and the equipment necessary to run TAP on a much larger scale. With these exceptions, the same policies continue to guide the operation of TAP today.

As one aspect of TAP's commitment to financial accountability, TAP staff members corresponded regularly with monastery administrators in India to make sure donations were well spent. Rinpoche created a form in Tibetan requesting that every donation be acknowledged and asking for a full accounting of expenditures, accompanied by receipts. Monasteries were asked to include photographs of ceremonies and other events supported by TNMC and TAP donations. Fortunately, the refugees were gaining familiarity

*The Dharma teachings are transmitted from one generation to the next in the
close-knit environment of a small monastery.*

with Indian language and bureaucracy. Many monasteries and religious centers now had bank accounts and knew how to perform the necessary transactions, so that donations could be traced and reported in a more business-like way.

SUCCESSES AND FAILURES

At about the same time as its formal incorporation late in 1974, TAP established a new office at the Dharma Press facilities in Emeryville, run by five volunteers. A series of benefit dinners held during the last quarter of 1974 raised over $10,000. Most of these funds went to support construction of Zangdog Palri, a large Nyingma monastery being built in southern India. Rinpoche also invited his students to contribute to the construction of the monastery directly.

In the second quarter of 1975 TAP sponsored six more benefits, including a day-long crafts fair in San Mateo. Later in the year, TAP hosted a series of dinner parties at the Institute, each attended by thirty to forty people. In May, Rinpoche participated in a special event to benefit TAP programs: a two-day dialogue among Eastern meditation teachers and Western psychologists called "The Tibetan Approach to Emotional Balance." The program, held at the University of Southern California, was attended by over two hundred health professionals, and tapes were distributed to hundreds more. All proceeds went to TAP.

In the last quarter of 1975, TAP organized another series of benefit programs, including piano concerts and a slide show by a scholar from the University of California at Berkeley on his recent journey to Nepal, where he had worked on preserving Tibetan texts on microfilm.

The projects initiated with these funds often encountered unanticipated difficulties. For instance, at one point TAP worked with Catholic Relief Services to send the refugees in India a huge crate of compressed clothing. When it arrived, none of the refugees could pay the duty on such a large shipment, and it had to be returned.

Early in 1975, with the refugees experiencing severe food shortages resulting from widespread crop failures in India, TAP secured the donation of a large stock of civil defense survival biscuits from Los Angeles bomb shelters. These supplies became the nucleus of a large shipment of food for the refugee communities. Catholic Relief Services agreed to match TAP's food contribution, and an organization called World Vision also offered support. TAP raised the funds necessary to cover the costs of shipping the donated food. That summer eighteen tons of food were shipped, with the National Guard assisting by trucking the crates to San Pedro Harbor. In the end, however, these strenuous efforts yielded limited results. Although the food arrived successfully, it did not keep well in the Indian heat, and much of it had to be discarded.

While such setbacks were frustrating to TAP's inexperienced staff, they also offered valuable lessons in the importance of thinking through every aspect of a project. At the same time, each new contact with the Tibetan refugees was a reminder that TAP's work had value beyond its worth as a simple humanitarian gesture. The Buddhist teachings that Rinpoche's students were studying and practicing had emerged out of a rich cultural context. Now that tradition was threatened with extinction. Unless the heritage of Tibet could be maintained and transmitted to the next generation, the wisdom that Tibet had preserved intact for so long might be lost to the world.

TIBETAN PEN FRIENDS

Could you help these people? They need food and clothes.

Just $10 each month can support a Tibetan refugee.

TIBETAN AID PROJECT 2425 Hillside Ave.

Berkeley, CA 94704 (415) 548-5407

CHAPTER FOUR

THE PEN FRIEND PROGRAM

Soon after Tarthang Tulku settled in America, he made a list of some of the lamas he knew in India and Nepal and asked students to take responsibility for their support. The students were asked to send ten dollars a month, and were encouraged to enclose with the money a letter sharing any personal thoughts or questions they might have. The amount sent was small, but often it was sufficient for covering the refugee's basic needs. In this way recipients could continue with their studies and their religious practice.

The letters the American students received in return were alive with a sense of determination and vigor, as well as deep faith. Many students found themselves moved by this contact with highly educated Dharma practitioners, individuals who had risked all that they had to make the journey out of Tibet and into freedom.

Over the next few months, the Pen Friend Program, as it came to be called, took on more substance. The number of letters received grew rapidly, and Rinpoche assigned one of his students the responsibility for coordinating communication, responding to the refugees' special needs or requests, and helping to resolve problems. Letters written in Tibetan were passed on to Rinpoche, who somehow found time to answer many of them. (For selections from this correspondence, see *Letters of Hope*, Dharma Publishing, 1997).

Problems with the exchange of letters were frequent. The mails were far from being reliable, and not every letter reached its destination. Sometimes a lama living in a camp would move unexpectedly, leaving no trace. At other times, the need for the refugee to find a translator meant that there were long delays and gaps in the correspondence. Still, friendships soon began to form. Rinpoche's students learned that small acts of generosity could have a tremendous effect on the lives of others. At the same time, their contact with devoted practitioners raised in an atmosphere of faith deepened their own resolve to put the teachings into practice.

THE PROGRAM EXPANDS

As word spread in the Tibetan exile community that Western students of

Opposite: One of three posters produced by the Tibetan Aid Project as a way of calling attention to the desperate need for help among the Tibetan refugee community.

Tarthang Tulku were sending money to individuals, letters began arriving from unknown correspondents in the resettlement camps—at first a trickle, then a stream. Westerners traveling in India and Nepal found themselves answering questions about the program and collecting information from many individuals who hoped that they too could receive assistance.

Over the next year or two the program grew at a startling pace. Those already being sponsored started sending names of family members and friends, asking TAP to find pen friends for them as well. The Tibetans requesting support ranged from orphaned children to the elderly, from tulkus and lamas to individual monks and nuns and families of ten or more. Looking for ways to meet their needs, TAP began requesting them to provide photographs to help their Western pen friends get a sense of the person they were sponsoring.

The letters sent by refugees wishing for a pen friend were often little more than simple reports of their daily activities or situations. Even so, they could bring tears to the eyes:

I completed my higher secondary studies and began teacher training last year in order to serve our small brothers and sisters. But there are great difficulties. My parents can't help me as they are working on roads and depend for their livelihood on this little earning. I hope you will do your best to find a friend who can help me finish my training.

Often initial requests from refugees asked for medical assistance:

I have just finished my annual school examinations, and I have done well. Due to the rains and my hard efforts in studies, I am now afflicted with TB. Should it be convenient to you, I shall be very much thankful if you could send some TB medicines and also some vitamins.

In other cases they spoke of still more fundamental needs:

I am well and doing my best with the kids in school, and with the sanitary problem. I dug eight latrines with financial help from a Dutch lady. Now the pits are full and I covered them up. The lady says she has no more money. So as soon as I could cash your cheque, which usually takes two to three months, I will dig a few pits wherever it is necessary. That is for sure.

To the best of their ability, the small community of students forming around Tarthang Tulku tried to respond. Most of the students did not have enough funds to support more than one pen friend, so other potential donors were recruited.

One way to expand the base of Western sponsors was to publicize the program. Working with graphic artists who volunteered their efforts, TAP designed three black and white posters, one of which is shown at the beginning of this chapter. Each poster followed the same format: row after row of photographs of Tibetan refugees, whose warmth and dignity could be seen even when the poses were stiff and formal. Printed by Dharma Press, the posters were placed at schools, in buses, and in

community centers throughout Berkeley and Oakland. In time they were sent to friends in other parts of the country to post in appropriate locations. In this way, people in dozens of cities had the opportunity to learn of the Pen Friend Program and to participate in supporting the refugees.

Through these efforts pen friends by the hundreds began to sponsor Tibetans. Some contacted TAP to offer their time and talents. Most Westerners still knew little about the riches of the Tibetan heritage, but the situation of the refugees spoke to people's hearts, awakening their generosity and good will.

TIBETAN PEN FRIENDS

Many sponsors seemed to derive a strong sense of satisfaction from this person-to-person exchange. In letters to TAP describing their correspondence, they often spoke of how much they valued the opportunity to make a difference in someone's life and connect with an individual from a different culture.

As one sponsor put it, "It seems to me that I am the real beneficiary of this program, not my Pen Friend."

An early letter to TAP reflects this feeling well:

My pen friend and I have each exchanged three short letters, concise

and honest. I know that the money that I have sent him has been wisely spent. And I think I can feel his prayers—a wonderful non-verbal experience from which I feel that I am receiving more than I am giving.

Similar letters came in to TAP month after month.

Often the contacts that sprang up between pen friends in this way continued long after TAP had ceased to serve as intermediary. Tibetans who are now fully independent still recall with great warmth and gratitude the aid they received in those early years. For many, it was the key to survival.

"Please don't forget me.
I am a Tibetan refugee living in India and
we need your support to live."

For further information contact:

TIBETAN AID PROJECT
Tibetan Nyingma Meditation Center
2425 Hillside Ave. Berkeley, Calif. 94705 U S A

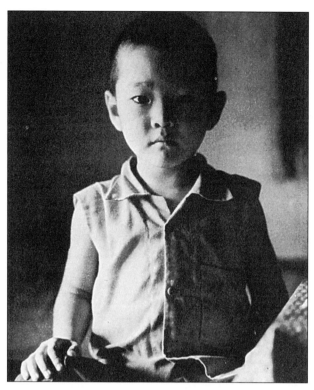

Above: Urgyen Yeshe Chongpei, incarnation of a lama killed in Tibet. His picture appears at the bottom left of the poster at the head of this chapter. Below, standing: Ven. Dzongsar Khentse Rinpoche, incarnation of Tarthang Tulku's root guru, who received Pen Friend Program support.

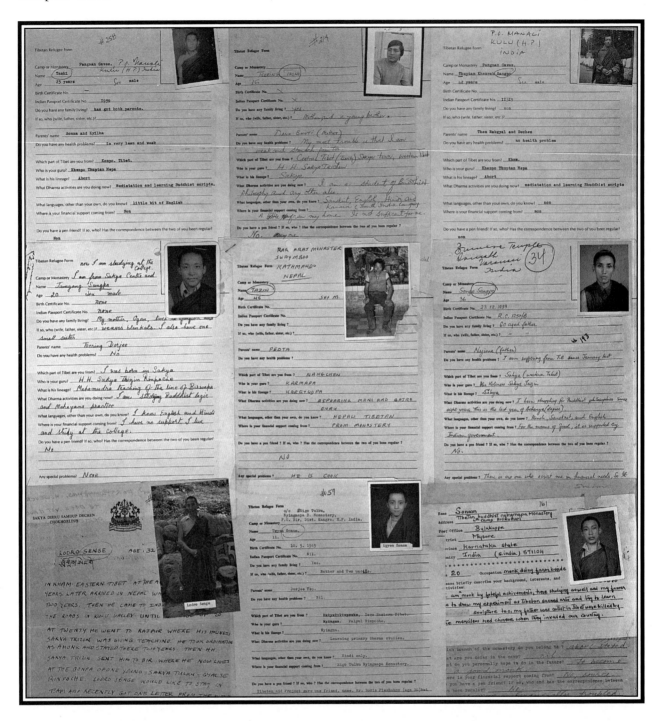

GROWING PAINS

As the Pen Friend Program expanded, there were inevitably difficulties and disappointments. Given the cultural differences, good intentions did not always translate into effective action. For example, many Americans had concerns about the health of their malnourished friends, and sent them vitamins. But Tibetan medicine follows a different paradigm from Western medicine. A Tibetan receiving a supply of vitamins for daily use might generously distribute them to every person in the village, so that the entire supply was exhausted

in just a day or two. Similar misunderstandings were common.

Other difficulties traced to the common belief among the refugees that all Americans were rich, as if they truly lived in a land where the streets were paved with gold. When an American pen friend missed a monthly payment, or had to send less one month than the month before, it was difficult for the refugees to accept that their donor might be having a hard time financially.

Sometimes Western pen friends began with good intentions but then lost interest, or else lost track of their Tibetan friends while moving, changing jobs, or

67

making some other major life change. For Tibetans, accustomed to connections that lasted a whole lifetime, this was not easy to understand. When TAP received letters from Tibetans frustrated because they had not heard from their donor, it could be difficult to offer satisfying explanations.

Language barriers were also a source of confusion. Tibetans needed translators both to read letters they received from the United States and to respond back to their donors. When whole settlements were corresponding with pen friends, one camp secretary might translate and write the responses for dozens

68

of refugees, giving the letters a generic tone that could be disappointing to American pen friends. But most people had ample patience and good will, and expectations on both sides gradually became more realistic. In some cases, connections were formed that lasted for many years.

Perhaps the most challenging hurdle in establishing pen-friend relations was transferring funds from the American sponsor to the Tibetan recipient. Sending funds from the United States to India or Nepal often required obtaining a bank draft and sending it by registered mail, which could add substantial

costs to the actual dollar amount being sent. India's notorious bureaucracy complicated even the most simple transactions. Americans quickly learned that the banking regulations in India could change quickly and without notice, so that what worked one time might not work the next. If a Tibetan name in its romanized version was spelled differently on the bank draft than on the Tibetan's identification papers, the banks would often be unwilling to cash the payment. Many refugees simply had no identification, while refugees in remote areas had difficulties in traveling to a bank that would cash the money orders

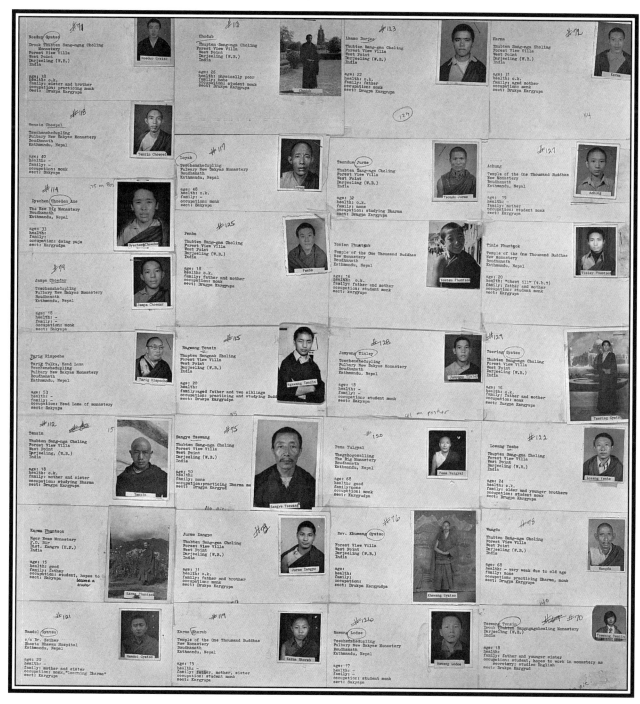

and drafts. To compound these difficulties, checks and letters would sometimes get lost or stolen, or be improperly delivered by the postal system.

Other difficulties came when a Tibetan pen friend had to move unexpectedly. Often TAP had to make extensive inquiries to find a new address.

Occasionally a Westerner would receive a letter in a different handwriting, containing new "instructions" for how to make out checks. In such cases, it was natural to doubt whether the money being sent was reaching the right party.

Over the years TAP experimented with various methods for transmitting

71

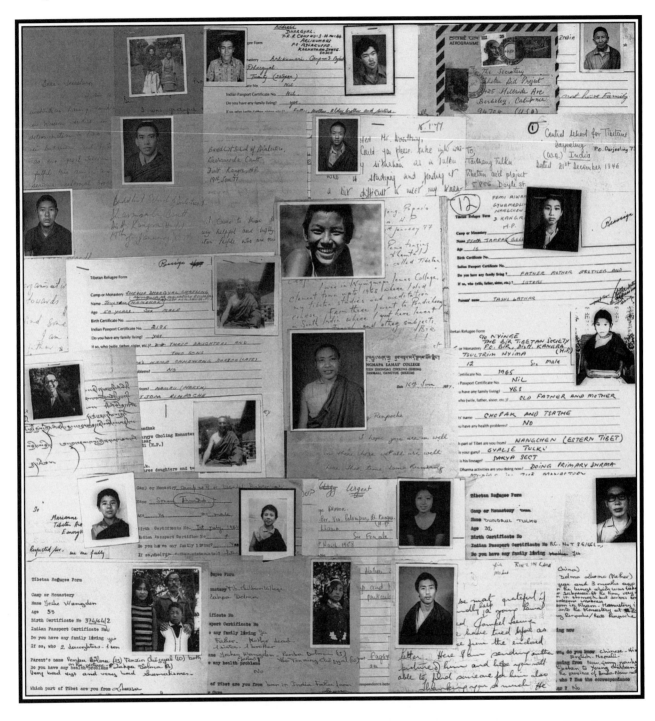

funds. In 1972, while visiting Nepal, a TAP representative researched the banking system to learn how it worked and how to transfer funds in the most reliable way. Travelers returning from India would offer their advice as well. TAP's incorporation in 1974 enabled it to send money to the refugees directly, and the TAP staff began to develop expertise in how to make the payments work. For a while TAP tried consolidating individual donations into payments that were sent for distribution to lamas receiving support from TAP in other ways. In the end, however, this system proved inefficient and time-consuming

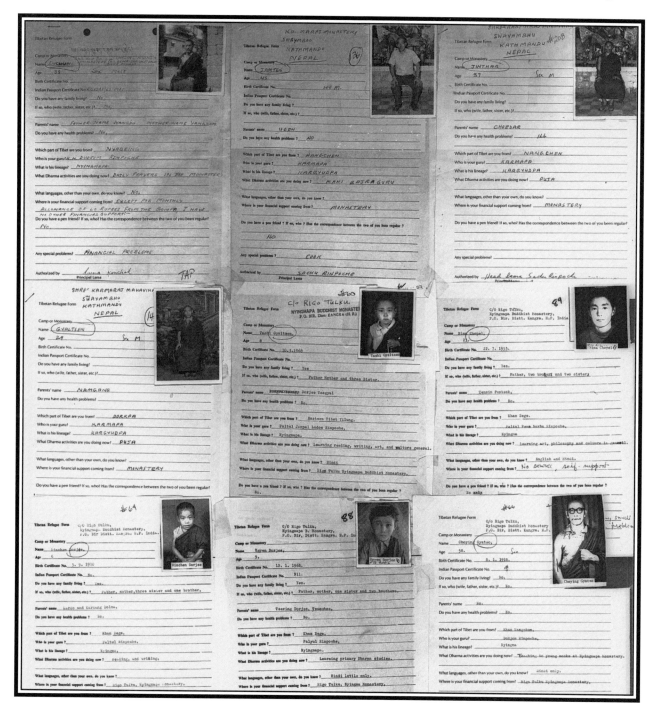

for the lamas, who had much urgent work of their own.

CONTINUED GROWTH

TAP records show that as of November 1974, six hundred Tibetans were receiving ongoing support through the Pen Friend Program. By mid-1977, TAP had files on more than a thousand American pen friends sending monthly assistance to refugees. These figures, however, are incomplete, since they fail to take into account the many donors who continued to send funds directly to their pen friends after TAP's incorporation. In financial reports published during the

1980s, TAP estimated the number of donors making such private donations at ten percent of the donors who sent money through TAP. It assumed that each of them donated an average of fifteen dollars a month. Recent contacts with some of the original pen friends, however, suggest that these estimates were probably far too low. For instance, one donor making private donations in the 1970s explained that her original Tibetan pen friend sent her a picture of his sister, requesting ten dollars a month in additional support for her. When the donor began making this payment, the sister sent a picture of her

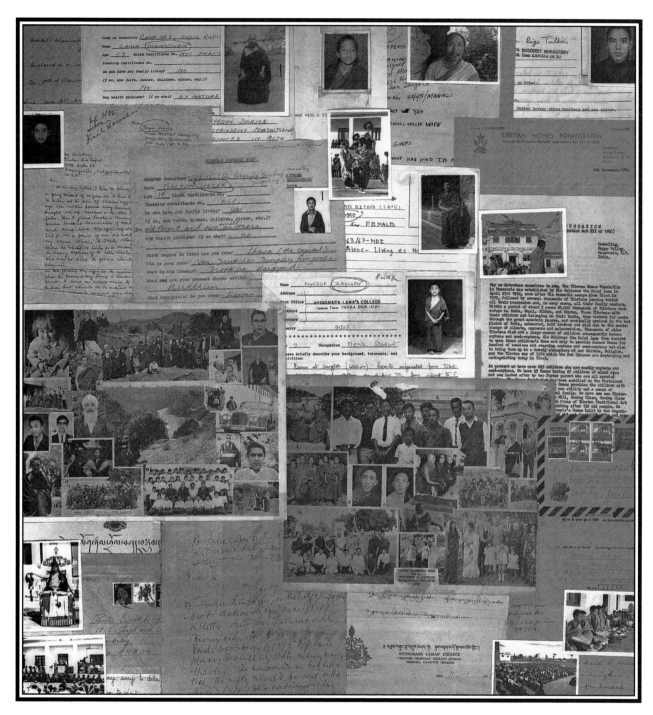

children, asking for more support. This pattern continued and expanded from year to year, until today the donor is contributing funds that help support an entire village.

Even if its financial impact cannot be accurately estimated, the long-term significance of the Pen Friend Program for the refugee community was enormous. Many lamas who received support through monthly payments from a pen friend when they were young are now leaders of the Tibetan exile community. One is the head lama of several important centers in Nepal, and others have made significant contributions to the preservation of Tibetan culture in their own right. Westerners who have studied with lamas in India or Nepal in recent years sometimes report hearing from their teacher that he was able to complete his training only thanks to the monthly support received from a Pen Friend Program donor.

PEN FRIEND PROGRAM FINANCES

During 1974–75 (the first full year after TAP's incorporation), TAP distributed a total of $2,869 to refugees. In 1976, that number increased to $11,883. Program income continued to be strong for the next several years, measuring $7,984 in

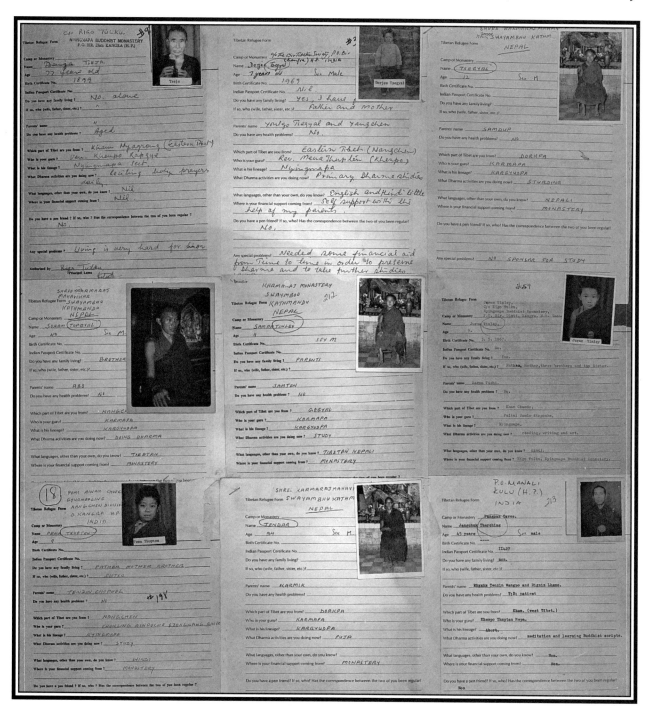

1977 and $8,100 in 1978. At that point, direct income fell off considerably, corresponding to a period of relative inactivity for TAP as other major projects initiated within the Nyingma organizations required attention and resources. Pen Friend Program income for 1979 fell by some ninety percent to $774; in 1980, the total amount received was $1,463. In total, Pen Friend Program income for the period 1974 to 1980, one hundred percent of which was distributed to refugees, came to $33,073.

As already suggested, however, this figure vastly understates the actual im-

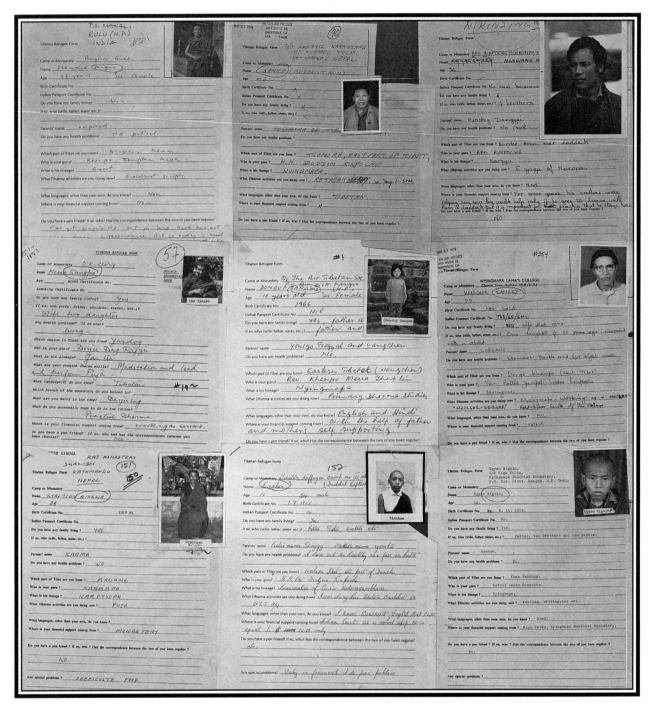

pact of the program. The TAP report published in *Gesar* in 1980 estimated that—given the substantial donations made prior to 1974, and in light of the ongoing flow of donations made privately and without TAP's involvement—total funds distributed through the Pen Friend Program to Tibetan ref-

ugees from 1969 to 1980 amounted to $438,000. Even this total is likely too low.

RENEWING THE PROGRAM IN THE 1990S

After 1980, TAP no longer collected funds for distribution to pen friends in

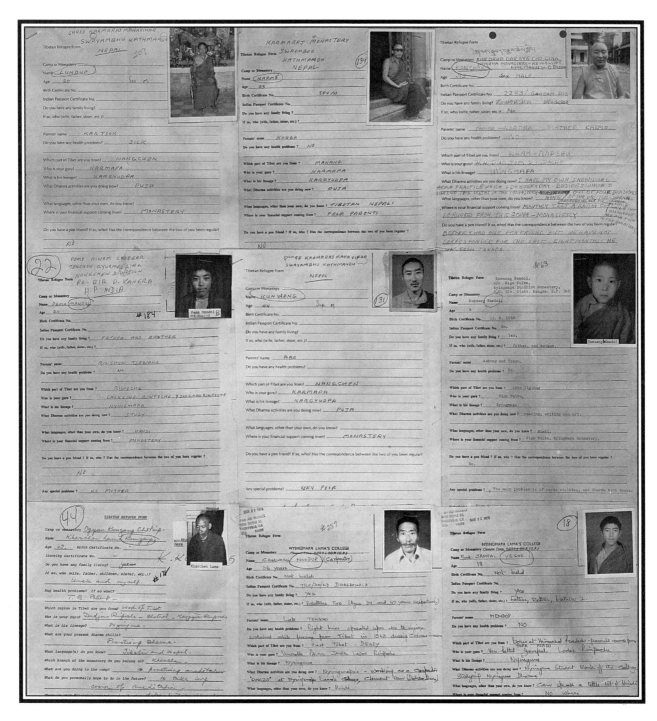

the refugee community. In 1988, however, the program was revived, with suggested monthly donations of twenty dollars. The new program focused on supporting students at shedras (schools for advanced study), monasteries, and nunneries. By now Tibetan culture and teachings and the situation of the

Tibetan refugees were far better known in the West, and the new Pen Friend Program attracted strong support. Hundreds of new donors enrolled.

In a change from previous practice, all funds contributed by penfriends now came directly to TAP, which forwarded

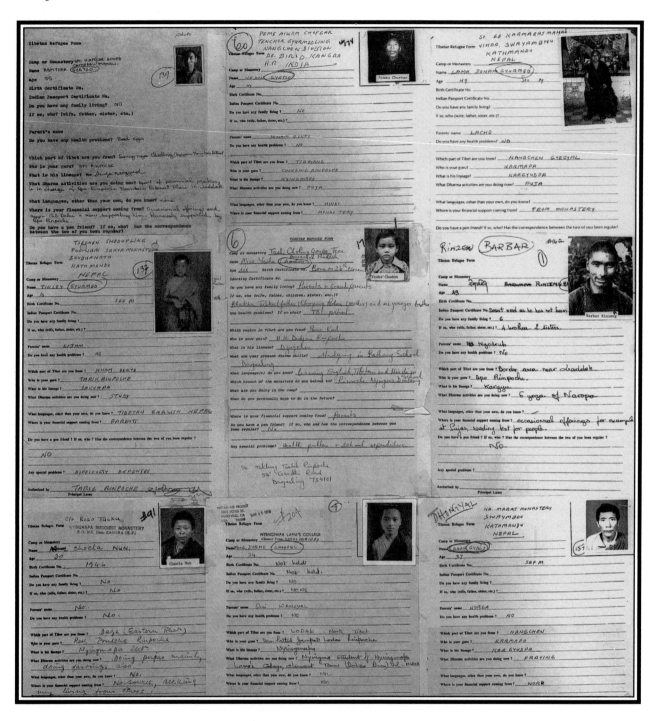

them on a regular basis to the monastic centers and schools in Tibetan exile communities. In turn, someone designated by each center or school passed the funds on to specific individuals. This approach allowed for keeping accurate records of how moneys were distributed, and greatly improved the chances

that funds would arrive with minimum delay and confusion.

By 1993, TAP was sending funds to over twenty monastic centers and shedras. As letters and snapshots arrived at the TAP offices in Berkeley in a steady stream, individuals were assigned donors

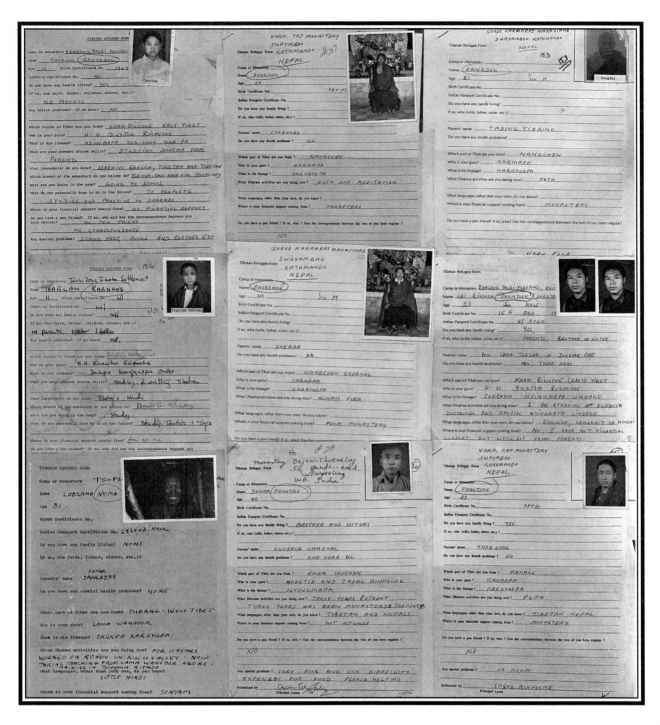

based on interests and specific needs. New friendships were soon flourishing, and Westerners again had the satisfaction of knowing the modest monthly sums they sent were truly changing people's lives and contributing to the preservation of a culture with much to offer the world.

After operating successfully for several years, the Pen Friend Program was discontinued in 1995. Under the system that replaced it, the monasteries, nunneries, and schools themselves took full responsibility for distributing funds among practitioners and students, based on their own evaluations of the needs

81

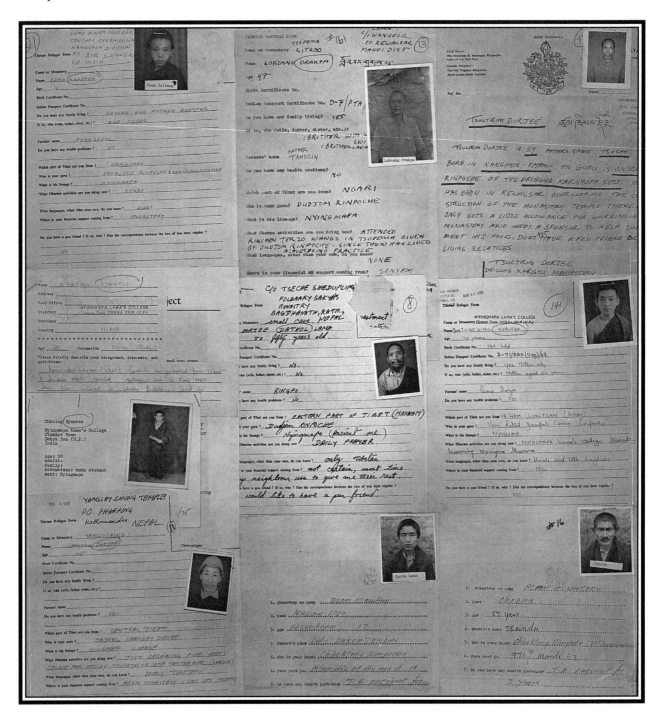

and circumstances of the individuals for whom they were responsible. For some donors, this new approach lacked the sense of personal contact that had been so meaningful in the past, but the new approach had major advantages. In the past, there had been concerns about unequal treatment of individuals based on factors over which the Tibetan pen friends had no control. Now such problems no longer arose. At the same time, the new program helped donors appreciate more fully that their contributions were vital in helping to shape a larger vision: the preservation of Tibetan culture as a whole.

Tibetan Aid Project

Support a Tradition of Compassion, Wisdom, and Peace

Compassion

The Tibetan Aid Project (TAP) Needs Your Help

For over 20 years the Tibetan Aid Project has been dedicated to preserving the Tibetan tradition of compassion, wisdom and peace. TAP's 1990 goals renew its commitment to the Tibetan people by aiding 150 additional monks, nuns and lay people through its penfriend program and by sponsoring 1500 participants for the 1990 Ceremonies for World Peace at the site of Buddha's enlightenment.

* * *

Protected behind the Himalayas for centuries, the Tibetan people developed a culture deeply compassionate and attuned harmoniously to all living things.

Out of reverence towards higher learning, thousands of Buddhist monasteries became scholastic centers devoted to exploring human awareness, developing wisdom, and creating richly inspiring art.

Though uprooted from their homeland by recent historical events, many Tibetans have set aside personal concerns to rebuild their culture. New monasteries in India, Nepal, Bhutan and Sikkim testify to the strength of their efforts. With your help they can accomplish far more.

We are fortunate that Tibetans have come into the modern world. With them they bring a living wisdom tradition that offers ways to penetrate the root causes of human difficulties.

Wisdom

a lay Tibetan to remain dedicated to the tradition.

By supporting Tibetan culture, we can safeguard a treasury of teachings in a world groping for values and overshadowed by the rush of technology. The contemplative yet practical tradition of Tibet provides a deeply-needed counterbalance to the pressures of our modern world.

Many Westerners have begun to appreciate the capacity of Buddhist thought to open new dimensions of inquiry. Inspiring a comprehensive investigation of human consciousness, the Tibetan tradition brings with it a wealth of knowledge.

People-to-People Support Since 1969

The Tibetan Aid Project has tried to aid Tibetans' efforts to rebuild their culture by linking over 2000 Westerners and Tibetans as penfriends, by providing medical assistance, food and clothing, and by sending educational materials to centers preserving Tibet's major lineages and schools of thought.

With assistance this people-to-people friendship program can continue. Your donations can enable a young student to receive teachings, an aged lama or nun to continue their studies, or

Tibetan Aid Project: Two Goals for 1990

Tibetan Penfriend Program Offers Monthly Support

Goal: 150 Western penfriends sending $20/month to:

* an aged monk or nun continuing studies

* a lay Tibetan dedicated to the tradition

* a young student receiving teachings

Ceremonies for World Peace at Bodh Gaya

Goal: Support 1500 monks and nuns for 15 days of prayer:

* $100 provides all expenses for one person

* $50 provides travel for one person

* $30 provides food for one person

Donations Made through Pen Friend Program
1989–1995 (Last year of Program)

1989

Individuals	$280
Total	$280

1990

Dechen Dorjee, Sikkim	$120
Individuals	$108
Total	$228

1991

Dechen Dorjee, Sikkim	$500
Ka Nying Shedrup Ling	$420
Nyingma Mahabuddha Vihara	$500
Rigo Tulku	$500
Individuals	$1,275
Total	$3,195

1992

Ka Nying Shedrup Ling	$900
Nyingma Mahabuddha Vihara	$3,200
Rigo Tulku, Bir	$4,200
Independents	$100
Individuals	$2,754
Total	$11,154

1993

Dechen Dorjee, Sikkim	$5,400
Ka Nying Shedrup Ling	$600
Nagi Gonpa Nunnery	$1,200
Nyingma Mahabuddha Vihara	$3,100
Rigo Tulku, Bir	$3,800
Taklung Tsetrul	$3,620
Individuals	$3,683
Total	$21,403

1994

Dechen Dorjee, Sikkim	$2,200
Nagi Gonpa Nunnery	$3,500
Nyingma Mahabuddha Vihara	$1,100
Rigo Tulku, Bir	$2,300
Taklung Tsetrul	1,200
Total	$10,300

1995

Nagi Gonpa Nunnery	$490
Independents	$8,995
Total	$9,485
Grand Total	$56,045
Total including Nyingma Institute of Nepal (see Chapter Six)	$128,757

Ima Zangpo

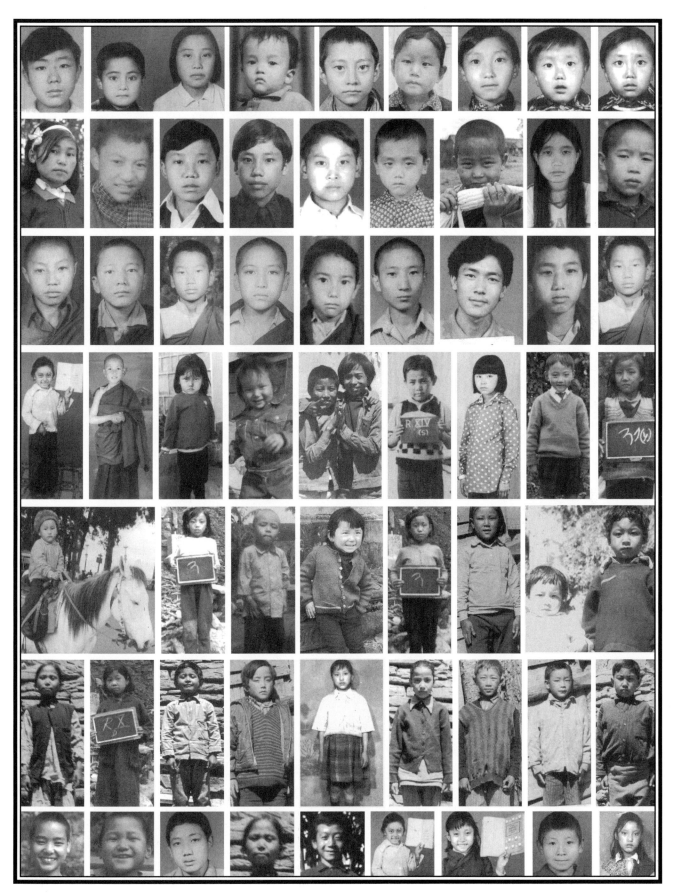

93

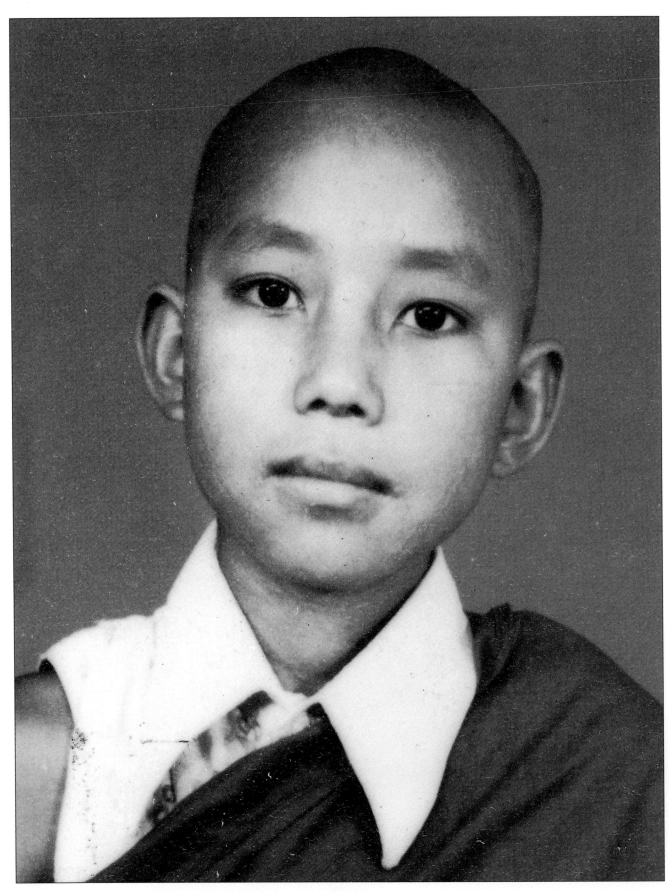

PART THREE

SUPPORT FOR
THE TRADITION

CHAPTER FIVE

SUPPORT FOR MONASTERIES AND SCHOOLS

By the mid-1970s, there could be no doubt that the regime that held power in Tibet was intent on obliterating its ancient culture. As noted by independent scholars (see Chapter Two), official Chinese accounts acknowledged that as of 1979 only ten Tibetan monasteries remained in operation. These ten institutions housed about a thousand monks and nuns, all that remained of a monastic population estimated by the Chinese themselves at between 150,000 and 200,000. The new generation of Tibetans was prohibited from studying Tibet's heritage, and even study of the Tibetan language was strongly discouraged by the authorities. Knowledge of the Dharma and all that it had meant for Tibet was fast disappearing.

In India and Nepal, on the other hand, the Tibetan exile community was making great strides. In the first years of exile, work on road construction had given Tibetans in India a way of earning a living in a new and unfamiliar culture. By the 1970s, more promising opportunities began to emerge. According to publications of the government in exile, H.H. the Dalai Lama and his advisers had sent gold dust and silver

bars to Sikkim in 1950 to be stored in case the need arose. In the mid-1960s, these reserves were transferred to a charitable trust founded to support the refugee communities, provide education, and establish religious institutions. This money now helped fund the resettlement villages where the Indian government placed the refugees as a first step toward self-sufficiency.

The resettlement communities were situated on remote tracts of undeveloped land. The first was in Bylakuppe, in Mysore State, South India: an area of more than three thousand acres located almost three thousand feet above sea level. Through hard work over the course of many years, the Tibetans were able to make these settlements into real communities that could work toward financial independence. Here families could put down new roots, and here too the monasteries and schools, so vital to the preservation of the tradition, could once more begin to function as centers of culture and learning for the community as a whole.

By the mid 1970s, many of the refugees were successfully producing crops

Opposite: Whatever destiny befell them, Tibetans raised in the old ways had faith in the traditional practices that had guided them from one generation to the next.

on resettlement land, as well as working in successful small-scale industrial operations. Tibetans living elsewhere often started their own modest businesses, relying on traditional handicrafts such as carpet-making, or on sweater manufacture and other forms of cottage industry.

Reports published in *Gesar* by students who visited Tibetan settlements during this time painted a mixed picture. On the one hand, it was clear that the Tibetans in exile were beginning to plan for preservation of their culture, carefully collecting funds to build monasteries, improve living conditions, and care for the young and old, the weak and the ill. Yet their resources were very limited. Projects begun with great enthusiasm often came to a halt when the money ran out, leaving half-finished structures that almost at once began to fall apart. Similarly, while the natural energy, good spirits, and alertness of the Tibetans were very much in evidence, many lived in extreme poverty. The community of monks, who subsisted on alms and offerings, were often the poorest of all. Disease and malnourishment remained common, and even after a decade or more Tibetans found it difficult to adjust to a climate and diet so different from their own.

Still, a small but significant part of the community was now able to follow the traditional practice of having their sons and daughters educated in the monasteries, where they could study the Dharma and invoke the blessings of the lineage on behalf of the entire community. In addition, in the years since Tarthang Tulku had founded Dharma Mudranalaya in Varanasi, Tibetans in various parts of India had established printing presses, enabling them to reproduce traditional texts they had managed to carry out of Tibet. While far from comprehensive in light of what was needed to continue the traditions, these efforts supplied the community of Dharma practitioners with at least some of the bare necessities for study and religious observances.

The keys to preserving Tibetan culture were the monastic centers, the traditional bastions of wisdom, education, and the arts. Early attempts by the government in exile to create a refugee camp for lamas and scholars—mostly from the Gelugpa school—proved unsuccessful. As the years went on, however, enterprising lamas managed to find the funds necessary to build monasteries and sustain the community of monks and nuns. The Central Institute of Higher Tibetan Studies in Sarnath, established originally as part of Sanskrit University, became an important training ground for scholars, and in the early 1970s the Library of Tibetan Works and Archives in Dharamsala began to offer support for Dharma study as well. Throughout the refugee communities, schools for the young, medical clinics, dance troupes, and drama schools were founded. On a small scale, the riches of Tibetan culture were being maintained.

EXPANDING THE SCOPE OF SUPPORT

Although the Pen Friend Program was the single major focus of TAP's activities during these years, more than half of all TAP's disbursements were applied

Children had to help their parents as they struggled to survive.

in other ways. A report published in *Gesar* for Summer 1976 lists examples: a thousand dollars each for a well at the newly established Nyingma Lama's College in Dehra Dun; to support construction of a large monastery being built in Bylakuppe under the direction of H.E. Penor Rinpoche; and as a donation to H.H. Gyalwa Karmapa for special religious ceremonies.

To meet the challenge of generating these funds, TAP explored various approaches, including a series of large-scale mailings. The brochures for the mailings were prepared with the help of Dharma Publishing and Dharma Press, which donated its labor. Today Dharma Press continues to print TAP materials at substantial discounts from commercial rates.

The first TAP brochure, printed in 1975, was not widely distributed, but its success encouraged further efforts. In the spring of 1977, TAP prepared a twenty-four page brochure (see page 101) that set forth the situation of the Tibetans, explained the importance of the teachings preserved in the Tibetan tradition, and outlined TAP's efforts on behalf of this endangered people and their culture. Mailed to some twenty-five thousand households, it generated over $5,000 for aid to the refugees. A similar mailing in 1978 raised another $5,000.

COVERING OPERATING COSTS

Under the guidelines established by Rinpoche, TAP could not draw on donor contributions to meet administrative

99

costs or overhead. Since TAP paid its staff neither salary nor stipends, administrative costs were low, and since it paid no rent throughout the 1970s and 1980s, overhead expenses were limited to the costs of mailings and a few miscellaneous charges. Still, these expenses had to be met somehow.

In the mid-1970s, Rinpoche addressed this need. He asked Dharma Publishing to dedicate to TAP a portion of the income from the sales of books in their new Jataka Tales for Children series (sample titles are shown on page 105). The Jatakas are important teachings in which the Buddha recounted to his disciples events from his past lives. The stories illustrate the workings of karma, demonstrate the power of selfless action, and show how to follow the path that promotes a happier way of life for self and others. The new series from Dharma Publishing adapted these teachings into picture books for young children that conveyed in a gentle way such universal values as generosity, patience, honesty, and friendship based on respect for all living things. Since these simplified versions of the original stories were not considered to be direct Dharma teachings, income from their sale could be used by TAP to cover the ongoing costs of mailing and other incidental expenses.

Because the Jataka Tales, which feature full-color illustrations on every page, are costly to produce, TAP and Dharma Publishing worked out an agreement for TAP to help pay for the first ten books in the series, in return for an agreement by Dharma Publishing to pay TAP royalties on these and all

As long as any living thing shall draw breath,
Wherever he shall be,
There, in compassion, shall the
Buddha appear, Incarnate.

—From *Mngon Rtog Rgyan*

Tibetan Aid Project

Telling TAP's story: the 1975 brochure

future Jatakas. This agreement worked well for everyone. On the one hand, TAP was helping to transmit a cherished aspect of Tibetan culture to the West; on the other, it received a source of long-term funding to support the continuation of that culture. A special source of satisfaction was that the books would benefit both Western and Tibetan children simultaneously.

The arrangement also proved financially sound. TAP quickly recovered its initial investment, and in future years received considerable sums in royalties.

THE TIBETAN REFUGEE SITUATION AND HOW THE TIBETAN AID PROJECT IS HELPING

"I am glad you all enjoyed my telling stories. You know, my dear children, even if poverty overtakes you, you can make yourself happy and that will make others happy too."
—*An old nun's advice to Tibetan refugee children*

Educating the public about Tibet: This 1977 brochure contained 24 fact-filled pages that introduced the Tibetan refugees and their struggle to preserve their culture.

For its part, Dharma Publishing gained a new line of books to present to the public, one that complemented traditional teachings. Now parents interested in the teachings of the Buddha had a resource for exploring Dharma themes and cultivating attitudes consistent with the principles of wisdom and compassion.

Jataka royalties covered the bulk of TAP's operating expenses from 1975 all the way through 1988. As TAP's activities expanded in later years, the financial significance of the Jatakas declined. Still, new Jatakas continue to be published, and even today sales of Jataka books provide TAP with a modest but steady source of income.

TIBETAN NYINGMA RELIEF FOUNDATION: FINANCIAL ACTIVITY
November 1, 1974–June 30, 1977

	Total To Date	*Nov. 1976– June 1977*	*1975– 1976*	*1974– 1975*
Receipts				
Donations	$50,770.66	$ 9,318.10	$21,280.46	$20,172.10
Pen Friends	19,727.78	8,899.28	9,467.00	1,361.50
Special Projects	5,473.02	–0–	2,735.00	2,738.02
Jataka Tales	1,418.62	1,418.62	–0–	–0–
Interest	1,910.59	350.76	899.88	659.95
Total Receipts	78,300.67	19,986.76	34,382.34	24,931.57
Disbursements				
Relief Support	51,530.59	16,373.00	25,184.00	9,979.59
Pen Friend Distribution ...	20,122.44	7,466.70	11,698.24	957.50
Register Letters/Postage ..	2,221.29	320.63	957.90	942.76
Office—Int'l Money Orders .	2,360.60	57.52	546.37	1,756.71
Nepal Dispensary	3,994.11	–0–	2,000.00	1,994.11
Promotion				
Brochures & Posters	1,728.48	360.65	452.76	915.07
Gifts to Donors	732.02	–0–	–0–	732.02
Transportation	373.73	–0–	–0–	373.73
Other	540.19	–0–	256.00	284.19
Food shipment to India ...	471.87	–0–	–0–	471.87
Total Disbursements	84,081.32	24,578.50	41,095.27	18,407.55
Net Excess (Deficit)	$ (5,780.65)	$ (4,591.74)	$ (6,712.93)	$ 6,524.02

In addition to the funds given to Tibetans by the aid project, the Tibetan Nyingma Meditation Center has given over $25,000.00 in an effort to maintain and sponsor traditional Buddhist ceremonies in all four schools in Nepal, India, and Sikkim; to provide general assistance, as, for example, the Dharamsala Clinic; and to bring and support visiting Tibetan lamas.

Combined with TAP, these funds constitute over $100,000 disbursed in the last two years. These efforts were conducted through the Center and are fully documented. Also, there are other special projects inspired by TAP, which cannot be measured; projects that send aid directly to the Tibetans, including hundreds of pen friends, who send their pledges themselves. Many supporters for the Tibetan Aid are Rinpoche's students, who he encourages to persist in the effort to relieve the plight of Tibetans and to foster the culture's preservation.

A TAP report printed in the Fall 1977 Gesar

Lessons for young and old: tales from the Jataka series

NEW MONASTIC CENTERS

When it came to preserving their culture, collective knowledge, and traditions, the Tibetan community in exile faced seemingly overwhelming obstacles. By some estimates (not those put out by the Chinese authorities), Tibet prior to 1959 had been home to some 600,000 monks and nuns and four thousand incarnate lamas (tulkus). Only about seven thousand monks and several hundred tulkus had escaped into exile. In a tradition based on knowledge fully conveyed only through prolonged interaction of master and disciple, this loss seemed almost irreparable. Could a new generation, separated from the cultural supports and environment that had sustained the vitality of this tradition for twelve hundred years, receive the training necessary to keep the transmission alive?

Whatever the answer to this question might prove to be, the effort had to be made. Like the monks who had fled persecution of the Dharma in central Tibet in the ninth century, the refugees carried in their hands the fate of the Tibetan Buddhist tradition. Now they set about facing up to that challenge. Guided by teachers with deep faith in the value of the tradition they upheld, they worked with fierce resolve and boundless energy.

Because its resources were limited, TAP had to consider carefully how it could best contribute to the refugees' efforts. One way was through support of the extensive building projects that the refugee communities undertook in the 1970s and 1980s. Most projects had to raise money as they went along:

When the funds ran out, building simply came to a halt. At such critical points, a small donation for materials could give a whole community the boost it needed to renew its efforts. Guided by Tarthang Tulku, the TAP staff chose its opportunities carefully, gradually learning to appreciate the value of proper timing and careful administration and oversight of donations.

EARLY SUPPORT FOR CEREMONIES

In the Tibetan Buddhist tradition, ceremonies are central to monastic life and essential supports for spiritual practice. The monks spend days or weeks preparing for a major ceremony, making offerings, purifying the temple, and intensifying their meditation practice so that they can participate more fully. Because such preparations incorporate sacred art and many aspects of liturgy, ceremonies also serve to transmit essential knowledge and skills from one generation to the next.

At the ceremonies themselves, participants chant prayers and read aloud from the sacred texts for days or even weeks at a time. The concentrated devotion of a body of experienced practitioners awakens the truth and power of the Dharma at a deeper level. By dedicating the merit generated, the practitioners are able to fulfill their vows to benefit others. At the same time, donations from sponsors provide the monasteries and the individuals who take part a source of funds that make it possible to continue with the daily round of activities and with study and practice.

A new generation finds its way in the world.

Turning a prayer wheel can be fun! Below: caring for the young

These monks are making texts in the traditional manner used in Tibet for at least six centuries. Wood blocks are carved by hand, then inked and pressed into paper (above) to create the image. Each page must be prepared using this procedure, making the process of printing both slow and laborious. Opposite: for Tibetans of all ages, sacred texts are the most prized of all possessions.

In the monasteries and schools for advanced studies, facilities for learning took priority over the personal comfort of students.

Above: Jampal Lodoe, head of the Nyingma Lamas College near Dehra Dun, leads a ceremony outside the newly built monastery. Below: musicians prepare for a ceremony.

Whether their accommodations were modest or more elegant, the refugees could legitimately take pride in what they had been able to accomplish.

The sponsor of a ceremony contributes daily offerings to participating monks and nuns, as well as offerings of tea and food, robes, or temple offerings such as butter lamps, flowers, and incense. Additional funds cover the costs of the ceremony itself. The donor specifies the purpose of the ceremony and how the merits generated are to be dedicated. For example, a ceremony may be dedicated to global peace, the long life of a teacher or master, the longevity of the Dharma, or to allay the suffering of others.

For the monastic Sangha in exile, the financial support that ceremonies provide is especially important, since most traditional forms of support are no longer available. But the ceremonies have many other benefits. Gathered in prayer, the Sangha strengthen their commitment to the teachings and their heritage. Their practice allows them to affirm their conviction that the timeless truths of the Dharma can heal and transcend all sorrows. Reciting specific texts ensures their continued oral transmission, traditionally considered essential to preserving the texts as sources of knowledge and realization. Finally, ceremonies offer monks and nuns a way to counteract the strong negative forces generated by the tragic events of the Tibetan diaspora and the occupation of their native land.

After arriving in America, Tarthang Tulku began sponsoring ceremonies as soon as funds were available. For many years, support for ceremonies came largely from TNMC, with TAP making smaller contributions and assisting with logistics and administration. Rinpoche was determined to support the traditions of all the major schools of Tibetan Buddhism, so funds were sent to monasteries representing the Nyingma, Kagyu, Sakya, and Gelug orders. Within each of these traditions, funds were further distributed among the different monastic lineages, so that a wide range of teachings and methods could be preserved for the future.

One ceremony honored within every Tibetan Buddhist tradition involves reciting aloud the entire Kanjur, the collected teachings of the Buddha in 108 volumes. Depending on how many monks participate, such a ceremony may last a few days or extend over a much longer period. Over the years TNMC and TAP have sponsored more than 316 such readings. For a list of other ceremonies sponsored through 1986, see page 138. For information on ceremonies sponsored through the year 2000, see page 139 and the tables at the end of Chapter Eight.

In 1977, Tarthang Tulku requested H.H. Dilgo Khyentse to preside over a very unusual ceremony at Bodh Gaya, where the Buddha attained enlightenment. Participants recited a hundred thousand repetitions of the Bhadracharya Pranidhana Raja, a prayer to develop enlightened qualities for the benefit of all beings. Conducting such an auspicious ceremony at this sacred site helped prepare for the restoration of Vajrasana ("Unshakeable Throne," the traditional name for the site of the Enlightenment). It was also a harbinger of larger ceremonies that would help shape the course of TAP's future activities, as discussed in Chapter Seven.

117

Butter lamp offerings convey the quality of enlightenment and penetrating wisdom.

Kanjur readings at Gyuto and Gyudmed Tantric Universities, important Gelug centers

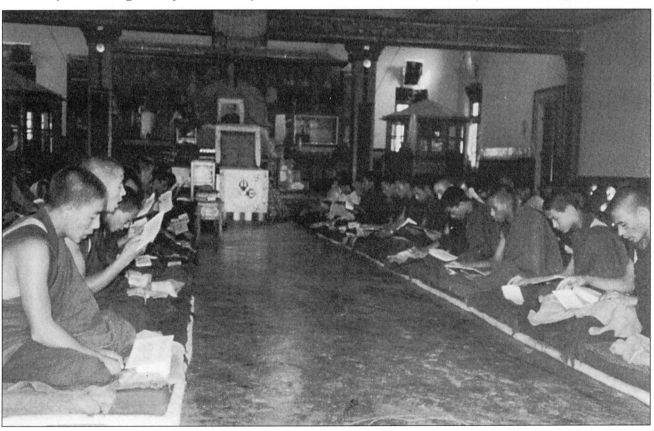

Kanjur readings at Drepung Monastery and Sera University, Gelug centers in South India

Readings of the Kanjur at Sakya Monasteries at Mundgod and Dehra Dun

Above: a Kagyu Kanjur reading. Below: a ceremony led by Thrangu Rinpoche

Above: a Kanjur reading at the Institute of Higher Nyingma Studies in Sikkim

Above: H.H. Penor Rinpoche prepares to begin a ceremony. Below: Kanjur reading at Pangaon Caves, led by Khenpo Thupten Mewa

Lamas in a refugee camp prepare torma for ritual offerings at a ceremony.

VISITS BY TEACHERS

As the exile community grew stronger, prominent teachers of the four schools began to make regular visits to Western countries. In part, this was to meet with Westerners whom they had come to know in exile; in part it was to make the Dharma more widely available. The visits also provided opportunities to meet with the few lamas who, like Tarthang Tulku, had settled in the West, and to offer blessings to their activities and their students.

The list of lamas who visited Tarthang Tulku in America during those early years included the heads of each of the four major schools as well as numerous other lamas, some of whom participated in projects that TNMC had

initiated and TAP supported. Among them were Khenpo Thupten, Khenpo Palden Sherab, Khenpo Tsewang Dongyal, Tulku Thondup, Dodrup Chen Rinpoche, Lama Jigtse Golok, Gyatul Domang, and Thinley Norbu.

Other visitors in the 1980s included Dzongsar Khyentse and Khyentse Sangyum-ma, widow of Tarthang Tulku's root guru. Whenever possible, TNMC and TAP contributed to the expenses associated with such trips.

For the Nyingma community, the visits by H.H. Dudjom Rinpoche and H.H. Dilgo Khyentse were especially meaningful, since both were revered and accomplished lineage holders of the Nyingma tradition. Both masters visited Odiyan, the country center and

125

Dudjom Rinpoche on his first visit, in 1972. Below: H.H. Gyalwa Karmapa visiting Padma Ling in 1974. Facing: H.H. Sakya Trizin during his 1974 visit.

Left: Dilgo Khyentse, a Dharma brother of Tarthang Tulku, visited in 1976. Above: H.H. the Dalai Lama during a visit in 1979, when he gave a public talk to a thousand people. Below: Khyentse Sangyum-ma, the widow of Tarthang Tulku's root guru, during her third visit to the Nyingma centers in the West. The photograph was taken in the gardens at Odiyan.

monastery whose construction Rinpoche initiated in 1975. Each gave his blessings to this major project. Accompanied by the young Zhechen Rabjam, H.H. Dilgo Khyentse also conducted a seven day puja at Padma Ling. For the students of Tarthang Tulku, these visits inspired their own Dharma practice and projects. For the staff of TAP, they also served as a reminder that the work of preservation had to proceed quickly, while such accomplished masters were still active.

INCREASED SUPPORT FOR CEREMONIES

A ten-year report published in the Spring 1980 *Gesar* (see page 136) showed that from 1979 to 1980, support for ceremonies almost doubled, to a

Monks rehearse for months to master the intricate dances associated with certain ceremonies. Left: Patrul Jampal Lodoe performs a ritual dance

Lama dances at Tashi Jong, a Kagyu center not far from Dharamsala. Below: rehearsal

total of $26,687. A more detailed analysis revealed that funds during this period had been distributed to thirty-two Gelug centers and lamas, thirteen Kagyu centers and lamas, five Sakya centers and lamas, and thirty-one Nyingma centers and lamas.

Total support for ceremonies continued to grow throughout the 1980s. Another report in *Gesar* that forms the basis for the table on page 137 lists donations totaling $128,327 for ceremony support through 1985. By 1986, this amount had increased to a total of $185,523, distributed as follows:

Sakya	$13,150
Kagyu	$27,028
Gelugpa	$35,335
Nyingma	$100,010

The tables on pp. 138–39 identify the specific ceremonies sponsored.

During the late 1980s, TNMC support for ceremonies dramatically increased. A report by TAP completed early in 1991 showed that through the summer of 1990 TNMC and TAP together had contributed a total of $504,420 for ceremonies. In subsequent years, much of the money previously donated to sponsor ceremonies at monasteries throughout the refugee communities was redirected to fund the World Peace Ceremonies (described in Chapter Seven). Nevertheless, as of 1996, total expenditures for supporting ceremonies, exclusive of the Ceremonies for World Peace, came to $606,156. See charts on pp. 140–42.

In the 1990s, Tarthang Tulku determined that the time was right to offer support for the Tongdrub Vajra Guru Ceremony, a traditional Nyingma practice in which hundreds of monks gather to recite the Vajra Guru mantra one hundred million times. Even in pre-1959 Tibet, assembling the requisite number of lamas and monks required for this special gathering had been difficult. Rinpoche contacted several high lamas about the possibility of carrying out the ceremony. Eventually it was performed once at Lake Rewalsar, once in Sikkim, and twice by both H.E. Taklung Tsetrul and H.E. Trulshik Rinpoche.

While TNMC expanded its financial support of ceremonies in the 1980s, TAP's activities during this same period were slowing down, as the energy of its staff was redirected to support major projects underway at Dharma Publishing and Odiyan. TAP income peaked at $41,095 in 1976. By 1979, it had fallen to $13,283. Staff analysis indicated that from 1974 through 1979, TAP generated approximately $127,000 in total income, including royalties from the sales of Jataka books for children. After 1979, TAP entered a period of near dormancy. A staff report in the Spring/Summer issue of *Gesar* indicated that TAP's total revenue for 1981 (not including private Pen Friend donations, which TAP had no way of tracking) had fallen to under $3,000. This pattern continued for the next several years. For the period from 1982 through 1987, TAP's annual income averaged $2,467.

In 1988, TAP once more began to expand the scope of its activities. Gradually it joined TNMC in sponsoring and funding a wide range of activities, as described in the next two chapters. The following brief year-by-year summary of the combined activities of TAP and TNMC from 1988 to 1996 suggests the remarkable range of Rinpoche's undertakings on behalf of his fellow Tibetan lamas and the larger Tibetan community, both inside and outside of Tibet.

1988

$75,446 for recitation of 100,000 Tara prayers at ten monasteries in Nepal:

Taru Monastery
Zhechen Tenyi Dargye Ling
Dapzang Monastery
Thrangu Tashi Choling
Maitreya Mandir
Shelkar Cho-de Gaden Lepshad Ling
Nyingmapa Wishfulfilling Center for Study and Practice
Nenam Pao Rinpoche Monastery
Samtenling Tibetan Monastery
Urgyen Tulku's monastery
    (500,000 recitations)

A portion of these funds were used to sponsor additional ceremonies at Palo, Tuthop, and Baro Kagyu Foundation monasteries, donations of prayer flags, travel, and other miscellaneous donations and expenses.

1990

Ceremonies $26,086

Tamang Buddhist Association, Darjeeling
Zhechen Tenyi Dargye Ling, Nepal
Ka-Nying Shedrup Ling, Nepal
Asura Caves, Nepal
Nyingma Shedra, Nepal; others

Monastery support $118,195

1991

$28,034 for eight monasteries, nunneries, shedras, and retreat centers in east Tibet, for preservation of Nyingma lineages and philosophical studies:

Traling Gonpa (branch of Kathog)
Tenpo Gonpa (branch of Tarthang)
Se Gonpa (Jonangpa tradition)
Lungkar Gonpa (Gelugpa)
Yag Go Gonpa (branch of Tarthang)
Dongzong Gonpa (hermitage of
Do Khyentse)
Tumpo Gonpa, specializing in
Payul and Nyingtig traditions
Do Gonpa, specializing in Nyingtig

1993

Central Tibet and Nepal $121,689

Tibet

Samye   Funds for monthly ceremonies (248 days of pujas attended by fifty to one hundred lamas); funds for reconstruction of Pehar temple.

Dorje Drag   Three years support for eighty-two days of ceremonies annually and for maintenance of forty monks.

Mindroling   Funds for repairs to the roof; support for monks, ceremonies, and offerings for three years. Gold for creating statues of Guru Padmasambhava, King Trisong Detsen, and Abbot Shantarakshita.

Tsering Jong   Three years support for nuns; funds for monthly ceremony offerings; funds to repair the temple roof; shelves to hold the Kanjur.

Shugseb Nunnery   Support for ceremonies and living expenses for nuns for three years.

Palri Offerings and three years' support for monthly ceremonies.

Nyepu Shugseb Support for ceremonies and living expenses for three years; sponsorship of paintings of the Dzogchen lineage.

Nepal

Ka-Nying Shedrup Ling One year of support for sixty students enrolled at the shedra.

Asura and Maratika Caves (powerful sites renowned as practice places of Guru Padmasambhava): one year of support for retreatants at Asura Caves; funds for rebuilding the retreat center at Maratika Caves.

1995

Nepal and Tibet $123,190

Nepal

Parping Monastery
Nagi Gompa Nunnery
Trulshik Rinpoche's Monastery
Parping Stupa Foundation
        (Sakyapa)
Ka-Nying Shedrup Ling
        (Losar Ceremonies)
Nyingma Institute of Nepal
Maratika Caves

Tibet

Tsongsen Gompa Pagse
Dorje Drag
Shugseb Nunnery
Deldre Monastery
Dregong Shedra
Dergun Wenre Monastery
Lhasa Jokhang

Mindroling Monastery
Samye monastery
Uru Shaye Lhakhang
Tarthang Monastery Shedra

1996

India, Nepal, and Tibet $106,753

Northern India

Mindroling
Sakya College
Sakya Monastery
Pema Awam Choegar Geumay Ling
Ngagyur Samten Choekhor Ling
Rigo Tulku's Monastery
Urgyen Thundup's Monastery
Dzongsar Khyentse's Shedra
Nyingma Monastery
Kangtrul Kagyud Monastery
other monasteries and centers

Nepal

Choling Rinpoche
Tenga Rinpoche
Yantse Rinpoche
Dechen Rinpoche
Chokyi Nyima Rinpoche
Urgyen Tulku Memorial
Rabjam Tulku
Tari Rinpoche
Ka-Nying Shedrup Ling:
        (retreat support for 10 monks for
        three years at Pharphing)

Tibet

Offerings for Dorje Drag given
at Bodh Gaya

Funds Distributed to Tibetan Refugees by Tibetan Nyingma Relief Foundation and Tibetan Nyingma Meditation Center January 1969–March 1980

Year	Ceremonies	Immigration/ Visitation	Relief	Penfriend Support thru Office	Sent Independently*	Yearly Total Dollars	Rupees**
1969	—	—	—	—	36,000	36,000	288,000
1970	—	—	—	—	36,000	36,000	288,000
1971	—	—	530	—	36,000	36,530	292,240
1972	—	10,226	782	—	36,000	47,008	376,064
1973	—	7,748	1,268	—	36,000	45,016	360,128
1974–5	—	3,000	6,316	2,869	72,000	84,185	673,480
1976	5,100	13,236	10,357	11,883	36,000	76,576	612,608
1977	12,770	—	207	7,984	36,000	56,961	455,688
1978	8,300	1,251	238	8,100	36,000	53,889	431,112
1979	13,860	10,953	266	774	36,000	61,853	494,824
1980	26,687	800	5,937	1,463	9,000	43,887	351,096
Totals	$66,717	47,214	25,901	33,073	405,000	$577,905	4,623,240

*Two thousand penfriends have been requested by Westerners over the past 10 years. Of these 2000 a few hundred have sent their funds through the TAP-TNRF offices. We estimate 200 people send $15/mo each year minimum for the funds sent independently to Tibetans.
**This total is calculated on a conversion rate of 8 rupees per $1. At many times over the years, the rate may have been higher.

CEREMONY SUPPORT: TNMC AND TAP
1976–1985

Gelugpa

H.H. the Dalai Lama	$600
Thekchen Choeling	200
for 15 centers	4,500
Ling Rinpoche, Bodh Gaya	3,275
Drepung Monastery	1,665
Dzongkar Chode Datsang	400
Gaden Choepel Ling	200
Gaden Jam Ghon	200
Gaden Tharpa Choeling	400
Gaden Thubten Choeling	200
Gaden Jantse Datsang	325
Gaden Monastery	1,565
Gelugpa Students Committee	890
Gomang Datsang College	1,240
Gyuto Tantric College	1,865
Gyudmed Tantric College	2,415
Loling Datsang	1,240
Sera Monastery	1,015
Serjey Monastery	980
Sermey Datsang	990
Shartse Norling Datsang	1,040
Others	1,100
Total	$26,745

Kagyupa

H.H. Gyalwa Karmapa	$830
Khamtrul Rinpoche	1,850
Dhazang Tulku	1,015
Dorzong Rinpoche, Tashi Jong	1,755
Ven. Ontul Rinpoche	755
Thupten Sangag Choeling	8,010
Kagyud Student Committee	640
Lama Wangdor	2,630
Thrangu Rinpoche	965
Others	875
Total	$19,325

Sakyapa

H.H. Sakya Trizin	$3,155
Khenpo Appey, Sakya College	1,930
Sakya Students Union	890
Khenpo Sangye Tenzin	765
Tharig Tulku	952
Others	750
Total	$8,442

Nyingmapa

H.H. Penor Rinpoche	$300
H.H. Dilgo Khentse	21,665
Khenpo Dazer	2,655
Khenpo Dechen Dorje	2,235
Dodrup Chen Rinpoche	1,685
Golok Tulku	1,115
Jedrung Rinpoche	815
Dzongsar Khyentse Rinpoche	3,785
Khyentse Sangyum	660
Khenpo Thubten Mewa	2,855
Shaptrul Sangye Dorje	2,165
Khetsun Zangpo	1,280
Nyingma Monastery Rewalsar	3,305
Ka-Nying Shedrup Ling	4,600
Nyingma Students Committee	1,440
Nyingmapa Mahabuddha Vihara, Dehra Dun	4,390
Pema Norbu Rinpoche	6,200
Tulku Pema Wangyal	740
Rigo Tulku	3,365
Ripa Tulku/Dorje Namgyal	2,030
Thuprig Dorje	825
Trushig Rinpoche	1,230
Taklung Tsetrul Rinpoche	1,280
Zangdok Palri Monastery	765
Others	1,430
Total	$74,115

CEREMONY SUPPORT: TNMC AND TAP
1974–1986

Ceremony	Total	Nyingma	Sakya	Kagyud	Gelug
Kanjur Rinpoche	88	31	6	14	37
Tanjur Reading	1	-	-	-	1
100,000 Tara Prayers	200	90	26	41	43
Heart Sutra	113	43	19	24	27
Vajrakila Prayers	47	33	8	5	1
Amitayus Longevity	29	13	7	7	2
Prajnaparamita	13	6	5	1	1
Guru Rinpoche and Dakini Pujas	17	6	4	7	-
Ye Dharma Mantra	18	11	3	4	-
Dharmapala Mantras	4	4	-	-	-
Hayagriva Mantras	29	20	2	5	2
Longchenpa Pujas	20	17	-	3	-
100,000 Medicine Buddha Prayers	14		1		13
10,000 Sitatapatra	10	1	-	1	-
Sixteen Arhat Prayers	3	2	-	1	-
Prayer Flags	3	2	-	1	-
100,000 Butter Lamp Offerings	3	1	-	-	2
100,000 Manjushri Namasamgiti	5	1	-	-	4
100,000,000 Mani Prayers	3	-	-	2	1
Stupa Paintings and Statues	4	1	-	3	-
Sampa Lhundrup	3	3	-	-	-

CEREMONY SUPPORT: TNMC AND TAP
1971–2000

Ceremony	Times requested
Kanjur Rinpoche Recitations	316
Guru Rinpoche Prayers and Sadhanas	90
Vajrakila Phurpa Sadhana	149
Tara Prayers	311
Medicine Buddha Sutra Puja	18
Heart Sutra	140
Amitayus Sutra and Dharanis	29
Ye Dharma Mantras	20
Hayagriva Sadhanas	33
Sitatapatra Prayers	185
Additional ceremonies requested	211
Total	1,502

CEREMONIES AND OFFERINGS OF BOOKS, AND THANKAS (TAP AND TNMC) 1969–1996

Tibetan Lamas	Ceremonies	Thankas to '91*	Books*
H.H. the Dalai Lama	$ 9,514	$ 60,038	$166
H.H. Gyalwa Karmapa	2,181		
H.H. Sakya Trichen	5,035	3,213	192
H.H. Chogye Trichen	500		
H.H. Dudjom Rinpoche	3,689	1,850	50
H.H. Dilgo Khyentse Rinpoche and Rabjam Rinpoche	30,997	28,994	970
H.H. Yongdzin Ling Rinpoche	3,268	796	50
H.H. Penor Rinpoche	20,315	17,949	236
H.H. Gyalwa Drukchen	9,670	13,412	166
Adzom Choktrul Pelo	80		
Jadrel Sangye Dorje	4,069	11,462	
Dazang Rinpoche	1,736		
Dodrupchen Rinpoche	6,445	8,059	384
Dodzong Rinpoche	5,409	9,532	169
Drigung Bontrul Rinpoche	2,452	50	
Trulshik Dezhag Rinpoche	18,200	19,064	366
Golok Tulku	2,887	11,561	50
Dzongsar Khyentse Yangtrul	8,150	6,507	627
Gedun Tulku	50		
Gongna Rinpoche	1,475	1,114	50
Jedrung Rinpoche	3,588	4,119	50
Tulku Orgyen, Chokyi Nyima Rinpoche, Choling Rinpoche	19,690	7,502	429
Khamtrul Rinpoche	1,850		
Khenpo Aped, Sakya College	4,200	6,845	225
Khenpo Dazer	2,420	537	50
Khenpo Palden Sherab	2,616	2,646	
Khenpo Sangye Tendzin	1,112	3,383	50

*Since 1991, books and thankas have been distributed primarily but not exclusively at the World Peace Ceremonies. Data on these ceremonies are included in Chapter Seven.

Tibetan Lamas	Ceremonies	Thankas to '91	Books
Khenpo Rigdzin Dorje	$ 3,000		
Khenpo Thubten Mewa	10,492	15,283	100
Khenpo Dechen Dorje	10,800	9,472	691
Khyentse Sangyum	7,412	3,044	
Khetsun Zangpo Rinpoche	2,910	2,527	292
Khocchen Tulku	4,715		
Ringo Tulku	21,197	6,746	461
Ripapa Tulku and Dorje Namgyal	3,981	8,537	100
Jadrel Rinpoche, SNS Monastery	6,500		
Taklung Tsetrul Rinpoche	27,515	6,109	241
Tara Tulku	735		
Tarig Tulku	11,634	497	150
Tarthang Choktrul Rinpoche	4,399	2,855	175
Tishen Rinpoche	678		
Tragu Rinpoche	3,720	965	66
Orgyan Tobgyal Rinpoche	5,215		

Tibetan Center	Ceremonies	Thankas	Books
Bir Sakya Lamas School	500	219	
Bumthang Tharpaling	4,547	1,164	167
Dapzang Monastery	850		
Drepung Monastery	10,805	23,482	200
Dzongsar Chode Datsang	652	5,970	
Dzongsar Sakya College	7,323	6,507	
Drigung Kagyud School	250		
Duddul Rapten Ling	500		
Dzongsar Shedra	500		
Gaden Choepel Ling	9,054	9,054	
Gaden Jam Ghon	1,062		
Gaden Jantse Datsang	3,950		
Gaden Mahayana University	1,000		
Gaden Shartse Norling	6,905	11,044	150
Gaden Tharpa Choeling	452	5,970	
Gaden Thubten Choeling	452	5,970	
Gelugpa Students Welfare Comm.	1,826	6,766	

Tibetan Center	Ceremonies	Thankas to '91	Books
Gyudmed Tantric College	$ 10,215	11,104	100
Gyuto Tantric College	8,489	10,945	150
Kagyud Student Committee	873		
Kagyudpa and Sakyapa	6,450		
Nagi Gonpa	600		
Nenang Pawo Rinpoche Monastery	673		
Ngor Monastery	500		
Nyingma Students Welfare Committee, Varanasi	6,412	$11,044	$ 271
Nyingmapa Buddhist Monastery, Rewalsar	11,825	8,278	167
Nyingmapa Mahabuddha Vihara, Dehra Dun	19,181	13,362	329
Orgyen Heru-Kai Phodrang, Rewalsar	1,000		
Padmasambhava Caves, Lama Wangdor	3,536	3,989	
Phuntso Nya Yab Choling Monastery	1,000		
Sakya Monastery Dehra Dun	4,875	3,383	
Sakya College	1,000		
Sakya Students Union	877	4,358	50
Samten Dechen Choling	300		
Sera Mahayana Monastic and Philosophy University	9,496	18,367	200
Tharpaling Shedra	500		
Shelkar Chosde Gaden Legshad Ling	678		
Tashi Jong	1,000		
Theckling Monastery	752	5,970	
Ugyen Wangdi, Monastery project	250		
Zangdok Palri Monastery	4,438	5,174	50
Nepal Monasteries: Stupas & Prayer Flags	6,609		
Total All Other Monasteries, All Four Major Schools,	167,168	124,802	
Totals*	**$606,156**	**$571,590**	**$8,149**

*Totals do not include TNMC donations of the *Nyingma Edition of the Tibetan Buddhist Canon* or offerings, support, and book and thanka distribution at the World Peace Ceremonies.

CHAPTER SIX

EXPANDED SUPPORT IN MANY LANDS

Through hard work, perseverance, and faith, the refugee communities were now increasingly able to provide for their own basic material needs. This financial stability enabled TAP and TNMC to focus on support for the Tibetan heritage, and in particular on the monastic and educational institutions that had always stood at the center of Tibetan culture.

In Tibet itself, new opportunities were also presenting themselves. As early as 1972, when the worst days of the Cultural Revolution had run their course, the authorities in Beijing agreed to restore some of the best known Tibetan monasteries. According to published reports, their intention was that these rebuilt monasteries serve as museums rather than as active religious centers. Yet the shift could be read as the first sign of a new openness. Over the next few years Tibetans cautiously began to practice some of the public forms of Buddhism, such as circumambulation and the offering of butter lamps. Since travel restrictions had been loosened to some degree, a few Tibetans were also able to travel to India and Nepal, where

they did their best to make contact with their family and friends. It became possible to dream that the glory of Tibet might one day be restored.

In the early 1980s, as communication between Tibet and the rest of the world continued to improve, Rinpoche received unexpected news: His mother, whom he had last seen more than three decades earlier, was still alive. The Chinese authorities had begun to allow travel to Tibet, and Rinpoche made plans to visit her. The trip, which took place in the spring of 1983, also gave him an opportunity to see for himself the situation in his native land.

When Rinpoche arrived in Golok, the province of east Tibet where he had been born, he found signs of suffering and devastation everywhere. Tarthang Monastery, where he had received his early training under Chogtrul Rinpoche and other revered lamas, had been razed to the ground. Yet there were hopeful signs as well. He met a few lamas he had known thirty years before, including his younger brother, Pega Tulku. He also met younger monks and nuns who sincerely wished

Opposite: The rebuilding of Tarthang Monastery in Golok, east Tibet, represents a rare hopeful sign for the future of the Dharma in Tibet.

A homecoming long delayed: Monks and nuns welcome Tarthang Tulku to Golok

to lead a life in accord with the Dharma. Although the younger generation had been raised under conditions in which Dharma study was impossible, their faith remained strong. Eagerly the lamas, monks, and nuns, as well as the villagers, asked Rinpoche if he could help them rebuild Tarthang Monastery.

Rinpoche responded quickly to this heartfelt request. Over the next two years, TNMC donated $108,000 toward building a retreat center and temple, including twenty-five rooms for monks who wished to undertake the traditional three-year retreat. During construction,

the burial place of Chogtrul Rinpoche, hidden from the Chinese and then forgotten, was rediscovered. Rinpoche at once arranged for TNMC to sponsor a thirty-three foot stupa for his teacher's relics, and provided jewels, silver, and gold leaf for its ornamentation.

In 1986, when Rinpoche returned to Golok a second time, he was able to offer two years of support for the construction of a shedra, a school for the study of philosophy. Completed a few years later, the school has 108 rooms, a courtyard, library, and temples. TNMC also provided funding for monthly ceremonies and offerings and support for abbots, supervisors, and staff, as well as ritual implements and living essentials. On a third visit, in 1988, Rinpoche was able to initiate construction of a Serkhang (Golden Temple), designed with 140 pillars and large enough for 1,000 monks. Upon its completion in 1993, TNMC offered funds for retreats, ceremonies, and staff expenses and established a fund to enable five hundred monks to participate in the Varshika, the annual forty-day "rainy season" retreat. To support study and practice, TNMC and Dharma Publishing donated two sets of the *Nyingma Edition of the Tibetan Buddhist Canon*, together with thankas and additional Dharma Publishing books. TNMC was also able to make more modest donations to nearby monasteries, and to support the renewal of Dharma traditions in other ways as well.

TIMELINE FOR REBUILDING
TARTHANG MONASTERY

1983–1984

Retreat center, temple, and twenty-five residents' rooms

Stupa dedicated to Chogtrul Rinpoche

Creation of ten thankas

Forty-nine day summer ceremony

Tara and Heart Sutra Ceremonies

Offerings to ten past teachers and lamas

Separate offering to Traling Monastery

1986

Completion of main temple, paintings, and statues

Sponsorship of ceremonies

Shedra construction

Creation of one hundred prayer wheels

1988

Initiation of construction of the Serkhang with facilities for more than one thousand lamas

Endowment fund

First-year expenses

Completion of the shedra

1991

Completion of the Serkhang

Rainy-season retreats for 400–500 monks

Two years of support for monks, including medical and pilgrimage expenses, four ceremonies monthly, and daily Dharmapala ceremonies

Sponsorship for copying fifteen volumes of Garlong Terton's teachings for the Yeshe De text preservation project

Donations: two sets of the *Nyingma Edition*; books, thankas, and statues

Cost summary

1983–1984	$108,000
1986	137,417
1988	290,000
1991	41,248

**Total 1983–1992
$576,665**

Above: Construction of main temple at Tarthang Monastery.
Below: Ogyen Samdrub Ling Monastery in Golok, rebuilt by Golok Tulku

Great stupas at a pilgrimage site in Golok, east Tibet: Guardians of the Dharma

AN EXPERIMENT IN SUPPORT FOR HIGHER EDUCATION IN NEPAL

The restoration of Tarthang Monastery was initiated by TNMC, which also provided substantial funding. Now that Tarthang Tulku was again visiting Asia, new projects and possibilities began to emerge for TAP as well. As the decade drew to a close, TAP once again began to take an active role in working for the preservation of Tibetan culture.

One major stimulus for TAP's involvement was Rinpoche's decision to found a Nyingma shedra in the Kathmandu Valley in Nepal, where thousands of Tibetan refugees had taken up residence. Tibetans had been making pilgrimages to the great stupas of the

Kathmandu Valley since the time of Padmasambhava in the eighth century, and ties between Tibet and the border regions of Nepal were extensive even before 1959. During the diaspora, several important masters settled in and around Kathmandu. A stable Tibetan community had soon formed in the area surrounding Bodhnath Stupa, east of Kathmandu: a sacred site long linked with the origins of Buddhism in Tibet (For an account, see Dharma Publishing's *Legend of the Great Stupa*.) During the 1970s and 1980s, close to twenty Tibetan monasteries were built in the area around the Stupa. At the same time, Tibetan lay people living in the area were able to develop some sense of economic security, so that they could once more support the monasteries.

The urbanized life of Kathmandu, its unstable energies intensified by the presence of thousands of tourists, placed great pressures on Tibetan monks and lay people alike. The traditional foundations for the monastic Sangha—especially the role of the Dharma as the thread woven through every aspect of life—could no longer be maintained in the same way. In Tibet, each village had had strong links to its local monastery, but in exile this well-ordered system could simply not function. Head lamas, already dedicated to providing for the Dharma education of their disciples and the spiritual welfare of the larger community, now had to think of ways to assure the material well-being of the monks and lay people who depended on them. The resulting strains made themselves felt in many ways. With Bodhnath and its environs evolving into a major center for Dharma activity, it seemed essential to support study and practice in any way possible.

One missing element in the Tibetan community in and around Kathmandu was the presence of a shedra, or school for higher learning. Traditionally, monks who qualified for intensive study would spend nine years or longer in training at such an institution. During this time, they received the education necessary to allow them to continue their studies on their own and to instruct others. In this way the oral lineage traditions for each text and practice were maintained, and Buddhist teachings were kept intact for posterity.

In 1988, having seen first hand the situation in Kathmandu, Tarthang Tulku decided to address this pressing need.

Working with lamas who lived in Nepal, Rinpoche purchased land on which he hoped the shedra could one day build a permanent home. In the meantime, he arranged for temporary quarters. The new institution was called the Nyingma Institute of Nepal.

Over the next several years, TNMC and TAP devoted substantial resources to the Nepal Institute. The Pen Friend Program that TAP had used effectively a decade earlier offered a natural model for providing support for the monks enrolled at the shedra. TAP set out to create a new Pen Friend Program for the shedra students. Soon all 108 of the shedra's monks had been assigned Western sponsors.

From 1989 to 1995, TAP was able to provide $112,163 in support to the Nepal Shedra, as detailed below:

1989

Pen Friends	$5,880
Other payments	241
Total	6,121

1990

Payment for rent	$3,960
Pen Friends	7,794
Total	11,754

1991

Payment for rent	$6,783
Pen Friends	10,484
Total	17,267

1992

Payment for rent	$2,000
Food Offering	1,000
Other payments	1,000
Pen Friends	16,800
Medical	600
Total	21,400

1993

Payment for rent	$5,567
Pen Friends	6,280
Food Offering	1,000
Total	12,847

1994

Payment for rent	$9000
Pen Friends	20,400
Medical	1,300
Other Payments	2,000
Total	32,700

1995

Nepal Shedra Rent	$5000
Pen Friends	5074
Total	10,074

During this same seven-year period, TNMC gave financial support to the shedra well beyond the sums that TAP was able to contribute. In all, the investment by both organizations through 1995 came to $460,446, not including the amount spent to purchase and prepare the land intended for the shedra's permanent home.

Despite good intentions on all sides, the connection between the Nyingma Shedra and the Nyingma organizations in America did not continue. In 1995, the Shedra relocated, and since then it has operated independently.

RESTORING THE TIBETAN HERITAGE IN ITS HOMELAND

In the winter of 1993, during one of his trips to Asia, Tarthang Tulku had the opportunity to visit central Tibet. The trip lasted for forty-five days, giving Rinpoche ample opportunity to explore for himself the situation faced by the Tibetan people. In a report published in the Fall 1993 *Gesar* and later sent in revised form to all TAP donors, he shared his observations:

What we saw was deeply disturbing. At each of the major Nyingma sites I visited—Samye, Mindroling, Dorje Drag, Shugseb, Tsering Jong, and Palri—the story was the same: virtually total destruction, and amidst the ruins a small community of impoverished monks or nuns struggling to survive and to reestablish their tradition. It was saddening to reflect that some of the greatest achievements of world civilization had been destroyed or had utterly vanished. Only at the most remote sites, including Shugseb and a few others, did there seem to be real vitality and a strong sense of devotion to the Dharma.

Everywhere I went, I heard stories of the suffering of the people in the years after the Chinese invasion. The authorities insist that these days are gone and that nowadays Tibetans are benefiting from new policies, but I saw few signs of activity directed at the welfare of the Tibetans: Most construction seems intended to benefit the Chinese or else to attract tourists. There were limited material advances, and countless reminders of loss and destruction, from the ever-present ruins to the stretches of barren desert that had replaced prosperous farmland and the hard lines that poverty had etched into the faces of the people.

Most of all, I was saddened by what I sensed in the hearts of the Tibetan people. On my travels people were always gracious and respectful, and offered what little hospitality they had available. But underneath, they have lost their spirit. They are dull and subdued, and suffer from paranoia and apathy. Something inside them is damaged, and perhaps even dying. Grimly concerned with survival, they simply do not care.

Possibly this can change. Within the limits of our own resources, I tried to offer material support at each center I visited, providing stipends for the sanghas there over the next few years, sponsoring ceremonies, arranging for repairs or rebuilding. But this is surely not enough. The Chinese authorities have done their work well, and I cannot say whether the heart of Tibetan civilization will be able to survive.

. . . Looking back on the months that I spent in Asia, I see it as a time of sharp contrasts. The joy of being part of ceremonies at Bodh Gaya was tempered by my experience in
Tibet, a land whose tradition and spirit seem broken. . . . Only forty years ago, Tibet was a different land, an inspiring realm of dramatic natural powers and profound spiritual expression. To see with one's own eyes that the whole civilization is simply gone is utterly astonishing.

Among the Tibetan Buddhist communities in exile and in the Himalayas, there is a sense of vigor and vitality, but here too an uncertain future awaits. Today someone who was sixteen when the Chinese took over Tibet is fifty years old; the next generation of Tibetans was educated either under communism or in exile. Soon none will be left who remember Tibet as it was.

Despite our efforts to support the Dharma and to preserve the art, literature, and cultural heritage of Tibet as a living tradition, time is running out. Young Tibetans are deeply patriotic, but their interest in the old traditions is waning. They see their future in learning about material things and the culture of the West. The irreversible momentum of these fundamental changes leaves me with a real question in mind: Can the rich heritage of the Tibet I was fortunate enough to know survive into the next millennium? *

---

* Readers interested in a personal account of circumstances in Tibet may wish to consult Ama Ahde, *The Voice that Remembers* (Boston, 1997). For a broader historical perspective, see Tsering Shakya, *The Dragon in the Land of Snows* (New York, 1999).

Nuns at Shugseb, in central Tibet

A DECISIVE RESPONSE

As a direct result of Rinpoche's visit to central Tibet, TAP (following TNMC's lead) began making modest donations to monasteries there. Its first donation of $1,400 in 1993 went to Mindroling Monastery; an additional $1,200 went to help other monasteries and nunneries.

In 1994, Rinpoche made a far more substantial commitment. He established and funded the Ka-Ter Foundation, and organization dedicated to supporting the revitalization of the teaching and practice lineages in Tibet and the Himalayas. The name derives from the Kama and Terma, the two major types of transmission lineages preserved within the Nyingma tradition. Soon after, the Nyingma Buddhist Religious Trust was established in America with the aim of supporting the work of the Foundation.

In order to fulfill its purpose of promoting and spreading the teachings and practices of the Nyingma lineages, the Ka-Ter Foundation planned an ambitious program. By offering support to rebuild holy places, retreat centers, and monasteries, as well as texts and practical knowledge and guidance, the Foundation hoped to help monasteries and nunneries revitalize the traditions they had preserved through the centuries.

The charter of the Ka-Ter Foundation provided that directors would personally determine what places in Tibet and elsewhere most needed support. In 1994, in fulfillment of that responsibility, officers of the Foundation, led by Tulku Sangngak, entered Tibet to visit Nyingma monasteries, nunneries, and retreat centers, distribute funds, and determine the needs and priorities. Funds were made available to five important holy places in the central Tibetan regions of Ü and Tsang:

At Mindroling, a renowned Nyingma monastery in central Tibet, funds were provided to create statues of the three founders of Buddhism in Tibet: Guru Padmasambhava, Abbot Shantarakshita, and King Trisong Detsen.

At Shugseb Nunnery, where Tarthang Tulku had been able to offer support for more than three hundred nuns in 1993, the Foundation offered additional support for twenty nuns to undertake an intensive retreat.

At Dorje Drag, another of the six principal Nyingma monasteries, the Foundation provided funds for creating large ceremonial-size thankas and fabric appliqué hangings in honor of Guru

Tarthang Tulku with monks at Mindroling in 1993: Celebrating a meeting across decades.

Padmasambhava, as well as support for fifty monks to remain in residence.

At Tsering Jong, the monastery where Jigme Lingpa lived, the Foundation contributed funds to rebuild the temple, set up a retreat center, and support twenty-five nuns for three years.

At Chongye Palri, the most important Nyingma monastery before the seventeenth century, the Foundation gave funds to aid in rebuilding the temple and to restore statues.

Holy Places for the Nyingmapa

In their travels in Tibet in 1994, the four lamas representing the Ka-Ter Foundation evaluated the condition and needs of hundreds of holy places, centers, and monasteries, and compiled a list of 205 Nyingma holy places. Although it has not yet been possible to provide support for each of these centers, TAP reprints the list here as a reminder of the work to be done. As a counter to the tendency of Chinese cartographers to give Tibetan names in a Chinese form, the names are listed here in transliteration (using the Wylie system), followed by a phonetic rendering .

1. lHa-sa Brag-ra-klu-phug Grub-thob lHa-khang, "Lhasa Dragra Lupug." The place where Nyang Tingdzin Zangpo, the eighth century disciple of Guru Padmasambhava, practiced intensively and achieved the Rainbow Body.

154

2. Brag-yer-pa Zla-ba-phug, "Drag Yerpa." Srongtsen Gampo made use of meditation caves here, and Guru Rinpoche and Vairotsana both meditated here in the eighth century.

3. 'O-brgyal-thang Tshe-bcu lHa-khang bShad-grwa-gsar-pa, "Ogyal Tang." A new shedra located in Lhasa

4. dBu-ru Ka-tshal mTha'-'dul gTsug lag-khang, "Katsal." Built by the great Dharma King Srongtsen Gampo in the seventh century.

5. dBu-ru Zhwa-yi gTsug-lag-khang, "Zhwa Lakang." Founded by Nyang Tingdzin Zangpo. Longchenpa received a vision in which he was instructed to repair this holy place.

6. Chos-lung-btsun Monastery, "Cholung Tsun." The official residence of Rahor Chodrak.

7. dKar-chung rDo-rje-dbyings, "Karchung." Associated with King Trisong Detsen's son, Gyalsray Mutri.

8. 'Bri-gung gZho-stod Ti-sgro, "Tidro." Site of practice caves of both Padmasambhava and Yeshe Tsogyal.

9. Bri-gung mThil, "Drigung Til." The residence of the Kagyu master Drigung Kyobpa (1143–1217).

10. 'Bri-gung bShad-grwa, "Drigung Shedra." Drigung Kyobpa Rinpoche worked at this center of education.

11. Gangs-ri Thod-dkar, "Gangri Tokar." Residence of Longchenpa.

12. Shug-gseb Monastery, "Shug Seb." A place associated with Rigdzin Chonyid Zangmo.

13. Shug-gseb sGrub-sde, "Shug Seb." A practice center under the guidance of Tulku Jigme Dorje.

14. lCags-zam Chu-bo-ri O-rgyan Nam-mkha'-rdzong, "Chubo Ri." Associated with the great siddha Tangton Gyalpo.

15. rDo-rje Brag E-wam-Cog-sgar, "Dorje Drag." Major Nyingma monastery founded by the master of Northern Treasures Ngagi Wangpo in 1632.

16. Yang-rdzong, "Drag Yang Zong." Holy place associated with the Enlightened Body of Padmasambhava; birthplace of Nubchen Sangye Yeshe.

Rekindling the light of Dharma: Tarthang Tulku celebrates a puja at Lhasa Jokang, 1993

17. mTsho-rgyal Bla-mtsho, "Tsogyal Latso." Small lake at the place where Yeshe Tsogyal was born.

18. sGrags-mda' gNubs-chen 'Khrung-khang, "Drag Da." Temple at the birth-place of Nubchen Sangye Yeshe, disci-ple of Padmasambhava.

19. Ngar-phug Tsha-gser bTsun-dgon, "Ngar Pug." A cave in Drag associated with the famed siddha Melong Dorje (1243–1303).

20. lHo-brag mKhar-chu, "Lodrag Kar-chu." Holy place associated with the Enlightened Mind of Padmasambhava and the birthplace of Namkhai Nying-po, a disciple of the Great Guru.

21. Gra-nang bKra-shis Chos-gling, "Dra-nang Tashi Choling." The birthplace of Longchenpa (1308–1364).

22. Gra-nang, "Dranang." The original temple built by Lumay in the tenth or eleventh century.

23. Gra-phyi O-rgyan sMin-grol-gling, "Mindroling." A major Nyingma mon-astery, founded by the great Orgyen Terdag Lingpa in 1676.

156

24. bSam-yas gTsug-lag-khang, "Samye Tsugla Khang." Tibet's first monastery, founded by Khenpo Shantarakshita, Lobpon Guru Padmasambhava, and Chogyal Trisong Detsen ("Khen Lob Cho Sum") in the eighth century.

25. bSam-yas mChims-phu Brag-dmar Ke'u-tshang, "Dragmar Keu Tsang." Holy place with numerous meditation caves, associated with the Enlightened Speech of the Great Guru Padmasambhava.

26. bSam-yas gYa'-ma-lung, "Samye Yamalung." Hermitage behind Samye where Padmasambhava created a spring flowing with the water of life and concealed longevity practices.

27. rTse-thang sNe'u-gdong Ban-tshang, "Neu-dong." Residence of the renowned Terma master Orgyen Lingpa (b. 1323).

28. Yar-lung Shel-brag, "Yarlung Sheldrag." Holy place associated with the Enlightened Qualities of the great Guru Padmasambhava.

29. Srong-btsan dBang-so dMar-po, "Srongtsen Wangso Marpo." Tomb of the first Dharma King.

30. Tshe-ring-ljongs bTsun-dgon, "Tsering Jong." Nunnery at the site of Jigme Lingpa's residence.

31. Tshe-ring-ljongs sGrub-sde, "Tsering Jong." Retreat center at Tsering Jong, residence of Jigme Lingpa.

32. dPal-ri Theg-mchog-gling, "Pari Theg Choling." Monastery founded by Terchen Sherab Odzer (1518–1584).

33. dPal-ri sGrub-sde Rig-'dzin Grub-pa'i dGa'-tshal, "Pari Drup De." Retreat center at Palri.

34. bSam-yas dBen-rtsar lHa-khang, "Samye Wentser Lakang." A temple situated below Chimpu.

35. lHo-brag sMra-bo-cog, "Lodrag Mawa Chog." Birthplace and residence of the great gTer-ma master Nyangral Nyima Odzer (1124–1192).

36. lHo-brag gNas-zhi bKa'-brgyad lHa-khang, "Lodrag Neshi." Site associated with the great Terma master Guru Chowang (1212–1270).

37. lHo-brag Them-pa Phyag-rdor, "Lodrag Tempa Chagdor." Associated with the Terma master Lhodrag Drubchen Lekyi Dorje (14th century)

38. Yar-'brog, "Yadrog." Monastery of Taklung Tsetrul.

39. lHo-brag lHa-lung, "Lodrag Lalung" Residence of Terma master Padma Lingpa (1450–1521).

40. sNye-mo, "Nyemo." Nunnery on the site where the eighth century master Vairotsana practiced.

41. sNye-mo-rdo, "Nyemo Do." Monastery associated with the Terma master Padma Lingpa.

42. Zang-zang lHa-brag, "Zangzang Ladrag." Location where gTer-ma master Rigdzin Godem (1337–1408) discovered the Northern Treasures.

43. Cung Ri-bo-che "Chung Riboshay." Residence of the great siddha Tangton Gyalpo (1385–1510).

44. gNas-phu Padma-nyin-dgon, "Nepu Pema Nyin Gon." Monastery associated with Terton Jangchub Lingpa.

45. lCags-phug dGon-pa, "Chag Pug Gonpa." Monastery associated with Rigdzin Godem (1337–1408).

46. Nya-mo-hor bSam-gtan Chos-gling, "Nyamohor Samten Choling." Monastery associated with Northern Treasures.

47. lHun-grub 'Od-gsal-gling, "Lundrup Osel Ling." Monastery north of Lhasa.

48. dPal-ldan gNas-dga'-dgon, "Pelden Nega Gon."

49. sBra-gur Dza-phug dGon, "Dragur Dapug Gon."

50. Gling-bu dGon, "Lingbu Gon." The residence of Zurpoche (b. 954).

51. sNye-mo, "Nyemo." The residence of the eighth century master Vairotsana, disciple of Padmasambhava and the first Tibetan siddha.

52. Dwags-lha sGam-po, "Dagla Gampo." Monastery founded by Milarepa's great disciple Gampopa (1079–1153).

53. rTse-le dGon, "Tsele Gon." Monastery associated with Dagton Wangchuk Dorje.

54. Khra-mo-brag, "Tramo Brag." Location where the precious teachings of the mKha'-'gro-snying-thig were discovered by Padma Ledrel Tsal; also a site where the Terma master Ratna Lingpa discovered treasures.

55. Dwags-po Byang-phyogs Ri-khrod bTsun-dgon, "Dagpo Shangsho Ritro." Nunnery and retreat place of the father of Bodpa Tulku (1907–1959).

56. Kong-po Bang-ri-dgon, "Kongpo Wang-ri." Residence of gTer-ma master Jatson Nyingpo (1585–1656).

57. Kong-po Brag-gsum mTsho-snying-dgon, "Kongpo Drasum Tsonying." Monastery associated with Kyabje Dudjom Rinpoche.

58. Kong-po Bu-chu Ter-gyi lHa-khang, "Kongpo Buchu." Built by Srongtsen Gampo in the seventh century.

59. Kong-po Zangs-mdog dPal-ri, "Kong Zangdog Palri." Residence of Kyabje Dudjom Rinpoche.

60. sPu-bo dGa'-ba-lung, "Puwo Gawa Lung." Associated with gTerma master Tagsham Nuden Dorje (1655).

61. dPal-kha gSang-sngags Chos-gling, "Palka Sang Ngag Choling." Associated with Rigdzin Chokyi Gyatsho.

62. sPu-bo Yid-'ong Khrims-gzigs-dgon, Puwo Yidong Trimzig." Monastery associated with Terdag Lingpa Namchag Dorje (17th century).

63. Byang Nag-chu-khul Dol-skya, Nag-chukul Dolkya." Site associated with Doltrul.

64. rTa-rna gSang-sngags-gling, "Tarna Sang Ngag Ling." Monastery associated with Jalu Dorje.

65. Nag-chu 'Brong-ngur-dgon, "Nagchu Drongur." The residence of So Yeshe Wangchuk, the ninth century disciple of Nubchen Sangye Yeshe.

66. 'Cha'-ru Nyi-grags-dgon, "Charu Nyi-drag." Monastery associated with the Terma master Nyima Drag.

67. lHo-ba-dan-dgon, "Lowaden." Associated with Nagpo Legden

68. Khyung-po Pa-tam-dgon, "Kyungpo Patam." Residence of Khyungtrul Rinpoche, the disciple of Jamyang Khyentse and Kongtrul Lodro Thaye.

69. dPal-'bar Thugs-sras-dgon, "Palwar Tuksey." Monastery associated with Dragngag Lingpa.

70. Rom-thang sGom-pa Grwa-tshang, "Romtang." Monastery associated with Gyalwang Dechen Dorje.

The eight great stupas of Kumbum, a major Gelugpa monastery in east Tibet

71. gSer-pa Ri-khrod, "Serpa Ritro." Hermitage of the Gold Seekers.

72. Ngang-zo-dgon, "Ngang Zo." Monastery associated with Sangye Won (1251–1296), the nephew of Gampopa and a Taglung Kagyud master.

73. Ne-khrab dGon-pa, "Netrab."

74. gSang-sngags Chos-gling, "Sang Ngag Choling." Monastery associated with the seventeenth century Terma master Tsasum Lingpa.

75. sGo-chen-dgon-pa, "Gochen." Monastery associated with Gyalwa Gyatso.

76. Gangs-ri-khrod, "Gang Ritro." Mountain hermitage associated with Menla Kunga.

77. Ga-grwa Ri-khrod, "Gadra." Hermitage associated with Karma Orgyen.

78. sDon-ne bKra-shis Chos-gling, "Doney Tashi Choling." Center associated with Konchog Senge Pandita, a disciple of Tsasum Terdag Lingpa (17th century)

79. rGyang-rgyad-dgon, "Gyang Gyad." Monastery associated with Ngagwang Tinlay.

80. 'Gam-phu-dgon, "Gampu." Monastery associated with Choku Sangye.

81. Ta-ka-dgon-pa, "Taka." Monastery.

82. 'Brog-mo-dgon, "Drogmo." One of the daughter monasteries of Dorje Drag.

83. lHun-po Ri-khrod, "Lhunpo Ritro." Hermitage associated with the successive incarnations of Terma master Tagsam Nuden Dorje (1655).

84. Ri-pha bKra-shis-gling, "Ripa Tashi Ling" Center associated with Ripa Lama.

85. Khams Ri-bo-che gTsug-lag-khang, "Riboche." Large monastery in Khams founded by Kagyu master Sangye Won (1251–1296).

86. rNying-ma Grwa-tshang, "Nyingma Gratsang." Nyingma center associated with Jedrung Rinpoche.

87. Ri-phug-dgon, "Ripug." Monastery associated with Ripug Lama.

88. Khyu-mo Ri-khrod, "Kyumo." Hermitage site.

89. Chab-mdo Karma-dgon, "Chamdo." Monastery of the Karmapa.

90. gNas-mdo-dgon, "Nedo." Monastery associated with the Terton Karma Chagmed (1613–1678).

91. Khra-chog-ting, "Trachok Ting."

92. mThong-ti Ri-khrod, "Tongti." Hermitage site.

93. sMar-khams rGyal-sras-dgon, "Markam Gyalsey." Monastery located in southern Khams.

94. Brag-g.yab Bu-dgon, "Draya Bu-gon." Monastery in western Khams.

95. 'Jo-mda' lHa-brang-dgon "Jomda." Monastery in Khams.

96. Sib-mda'-dgon, "Sipda." Monastery associated with the Nyingma center of Zhechen Tenyi Dargye Ling in Khams.

97. Khams-pa-sgar, "Kampagar." Monastery associated with the master Kunga Tenzin Ume.

161

98. Nang-chen Tshes-bcu-khang, "Nangchen Tsechu Kang." Temple associated with Aday Rinpoche.

99. Nang-chen Gad-chag-dgon, "Nangchen Gadcha." Monastery associated with Tsognyi Pema Drimed Odzer (b. 1828), disciple of Chogyal Dorje.

100. Gad-chag dGon-lag, "Gadcha." Branch monastery of Nangchen Gadcha.

101. Re-ya-dgon, "Reya."

102. bDe-chen-gling, "Dechen Ling."

103. gSang-chen dGe-dgon, "Sangchen Ge Gon."

104. Cog-rtse Bar-'gag, "Chogtse Bargak."

105. Chos-gling-dgon, "Choling Gon."

106. Chu-brgyad-dgon, "Chugye Gon."

107. Se-rug-dgon, "Serug Gon."

108. mDo-shing-dgon, "Doshing Gon."

109. Chos-'khor-dgon, "Chokor Gon."

110. dGon-nyin-dgon, "Gonyin Gon."

111. rTogs-phud-dgon, "Togpu Gon."

112. rNga-sgang-dgon, "Nga Gang Gon."

113. Nang-chen mGar-dgon, "Nangchen Gar Gon." Monastery associated with Garchen Rinpoche.

114. lHo-me Yel-dgon, "Lomey Yel Gon."

115. Zam-me-dgon, "Zamey Gon." Monastery associated with Chokyi Senge.

116. Tshab-sgar sKed-dgon, "Tsapgar Ked Gon." Monastery associated with Ketrul Rinpoche.

117. rGyang-yag-dgon, "Gyang Yag Gon" Monastery associated with Khekar Lama.

118. mKhar-chen-dgon, "Karchen Gon." Monastery associated with Lama Tharpa.

119. rNga-sgang-dgon, "Nga Gang Gon." Monastery associated with Nyima Tulku.

120. sTag-khyams Ri-khrod, "Takyam." Hermitage.

121. 'Brong-pa Bar-ma-dgon, "Drongpa Barma Gon." Monastery associated with Tsogyal Tulku

122. rJa-spar Me-dgon, "Japar Mey Gon" Monastery associated with Tsogyal Tulku.

123. Ri-pa Pad-rnams-dgon, "Ripa Panam Gon." Monastery affiliated with Gong-sar Monastery.

124. rGya-can-dgon, "Gyachen Gon" Monastery associated with Gyalchen Tulku.

125. gNas-rten-dgon, "Neten Gon." Monastery associated with the renowned Terma master Chogyur Dechen Lingpa (1829–1870).

126. rTa-rna-dgon, "Tanag Gon" Monastery associated with Sangye Yerpa.

127. rDzogs-lcam-dgon, "Dzogcham Gon."

128. Brag-nag-dgon, "Drag Nag Gon" Monastery associated with Dragnag Tulku.

129. Go-'jo Ra-khrid-dgon, "Gojo Ratri Gon." Monastery associated with Nyag-lha Jangchub Dorje.

130. sTag-mo-dgon, "Tagmo Gon." Monastery associated with Lama Lodro.

131. Ra-mgo-dgon, "Rago Gon." Monastery associated with Ramgo Tulku.

Branches of dPal-yul, a major Nyingma monastery founded in 1665 by Kunzang Sherab:

132. Ta-la-dgon, "Tala Gon."

133. Thob-ra-dgon, "Tobra Gon."

134. Bang-khang-dgon, "Bangkang Gon."

135. Kha-legs-dgon, "Kaleg Gon."

136. dMar-po-dgon, "Marpo Gon."

137. 'Bo-lo-dgon, "Bolo Gon"

138. bShad-sgrub dGe-'phel-gling, "Shedrup Gepel Ling."

(end of branches of dPal-yul)

139. dKor-khung-dgon, "Korkung Gon." Monastery associated with the late Tulku Orgyen.

140. sBa-bang Jo-dgon, "Babang Jo Gon."

141. dGon-gsar-dgon, "Gonsar Gon."

142. rGya-ra-dgon-pa, "Gyara Gonpa."

143. sPyang-khang dGon-pa, "Sheng Kang Gonpa."

144. Rang-gzhon dGon-pa, "Rangzhon Gonpa."

145. dNgul-ra dGon-pa, "Ngulra Gon-pa."

146. Tsha-ru dGon-pa, "Tsaru Gon-pa."

147. De-mtha' dGon-pa, "Demta Gonpa."

148. Klu-chung dGon-pa, "Luchung Gon-pa."

149. Sogs-lung dGon-pa, "Soglung Gonpa."

150. Klu-sug dGon-pa, "Lusug Gonpa."

151. Kaḥ-thog rDo-rje-gdan, "Kathog Dorjeden" Founded by Kadamapa Deshegs (1122–1192).

152. dPal-yul rNam-rgyal Byang-chub-gling, "Palyul Changchub Ling." Major Nyingma monastery founded in 1665 by Rigdzin Kunzang Sherab (1636–1699).

153. rDzogs-chen O-rgyan bSam-gtan Chos-gling, "Dzogchen Orgyan Samten Choling." Major Nyingma Monastery founded in 1685 by Dzogchen Pema Rigdzin.

154. Zhe-chen bStan-gnyis Dar-rgyas-gling, "Zhechen Tenyi Dargye Ling." Major Nyingma Monastery founded in 1735 by the second Zhechen Rabjam (1713–1769).

155. rDzogs-chen Shrī Singha, College at Dzogchen Monastery founded by the great Gyalsre Zhenpen Taye (1800).

156. Zhe-chen bShad-grwa, "Zhechen Shedra." College associated with Zhechen Monastery.

157. Zhe-chen sGrub-sde, "Zhe-chen drup-de." Practice center associated with Zhe-chen Monastery.

158. dGe-mang-dgon, "Gemang Gon." Monastery under the care of Zhechen Gyaltsap.

159. lCang-ma Ri-khrod, "Changma Ri-tro" Willow Hermitage, where Khenpo Thubga (20th century) resided.

160. 'Ju-nyung dgon, "Junyung Gon."

161. mKhan-chen 'Jigs-med Phun-tshogs Chos-sgar, "Kenchen Jigme Phuntso Chogar."

162. mKhan-chen Mun-sel Chos-sgar, "Kenchen Munsel Chogar."

163. mKhan-chen Chos-khyab Chos-sgar, "Kenchen Chokyab Chogar."

164. rDo-grub-dgon, "Dodrup Gon." Established by Dodrub Chen Rinpoche.

165. dPal-yul Dar-thang-dgon, "Palyul Tarthang Gon." Branch of Palyul Monastery; residence of Tarthang Chogtrul Rinpoche.

166. mDo-mang-dgon, "Domang Gon."

167. A-bse-dgon, "Abse Gon."

168. Dza-ka-dgon, "Dzaka Gon."

169. Ewam-dgon, "Ewam Gon."

170. Cag-bu-dgon, "Chagbu Gon."

171. Yid-lhung-dgon, "Yilung Gon."

172. Nor-lung-dgon, "Norlung Gon."

173. Brag-lhar-dgon, "Draglar Gon."

174. Gyang-kar-dgon, "Gyangkar Gon."

175. bKra-shis-dgon, "Tashi Gon."

176. bKod-sde-dgon, "Kodey Gon."

177. dByar-dgon, "Yar Gon."

178. Nyag-be-dgon, "Nyag Bey Gon."

179. A-nges-dgon, "Angey Gon."

180. sMyo-shul-dgon, "Nyoshul Gon."

181. Nyag lCags-mdud-dgon, "Chagdu Gon."

182. gNam-brag-dgon, "Namdrag Gon"

183. 'Byung-khung-dgon, "Jungkung Gon." Follows the Kathog tradition.

184. Rang-shar-dgon, "Rangshar Gon." Follows the Dzogchen tradition.

185. Jo-mo Khri-dgon, "Jomo Tri Gon." Follows the Dzogchen tradition.

186. rTa'u bKra-shis Chos-gling, "Tau Tashi Choling." Follows Dzogchen tradition.

187. A-se-dgon, "Asey Gon." Follows the Mindroling tradition.

188. Ke-ra-dgon, "Kera Gon." Follows the Mindroling tradition.

189. Klu-mo Rang-phul-tshogs-dgon, "Lumo Rangpul Tsog Gon." Follows the Mindroling tradition.

190. Chos-grags-dgon, "Chodrag Gon" Follows the Mindroling tradition.

191. Dril-dkar-dgon, "Drilkar Gon." Follows the Dzogchen tradition.

Monasteries in Nyarong:

192. lHa-ru-dgon, "Laru Gon." Follows the Kathog tradition.

193. Gu-ru-dgon, "Guru Gon." Follows the Dzogchen tradition.

194. rTsa-ra-dgon, "Tsara Gon." Follows the Kathog tradition.

195. rMe-ba Chos-'grub dGon, "Mewa Chodrup Gon." Follows Dzogchen tradition.

196. Phyag-phud-dgon, "Chagpud Gon" Follows the Mindroling tradition.

197. Ye-le-dgon, "Yeley Gon." Follows the Kathog tradition.

198. Gra-lag-dgon, "Dralag Gon." Follows the Kathog tradition.

199. Wam-war-dgon, "Wamwar Gon" Follows the Payul tradition.

200. g.Yag-'dra-dgon, "Yagdra Gon." Follows the Payul tradition.

201. A-'dzom-dgon, "Adzom Gon." Residence of Drugpa Rinpoche.

202. Khang-dmar-dgon, "Kangmar Gon." Follows the Dzogchen tradition.

203. Ru-ru-dgon, "Ruru Gon."

204. Ka-ra-dgon, "Kara Gon."

DHARMA SUPPORT IN BHUTAN

After returning to Nepal from Tibet during his trip in 1993, Tarthang Tulku visited Bhutan, a land where the Dharma has been practiced in accord with the teachings of great Tibetan masters for centuries, and where the tradition continues intact. In his report on his trip in the Fall 1993 issue of *Gesar*, he presented an encouraging picture:

My first impressions were of tremendous contrast with Tibet. Here was a healthy land: steep mountains and rocky canyons with abundant wildlife, a vigorous economy that produces a surplus of food for export, and luxuriant growth everywhere: lush jungles and miles of colorful rhododendrons.

The founder of Bhutan, the first Dharma Raja, was Ngawang Namgyal, the Drugpa Kagyu master who arrived in 1616 from Drug Sangga Choling in Tibet. The main official temples at Paro, Thimpu, and Bumthang are Kagyu. But there are an equal number of Nyingma practitioners, especially in eastern Bhutan.

They follow the Nyingtig lineage and the Loter (Southern Terma) teachings of Padma Lingpa. The people revere Padmasambhava, and among recent masters Dudjom Rinpoche, Shabtrul Rinpoche, and Khyentse Rinpoche are all deeply respected.

The young monarch of Bhutan is very impressive and dignified. His valley kingdom lies between two powerful nations, but like the Dharma kings of old, he is committed to upholding his country's distinctive heritage and to supporting the Dharma. He has been able to give his people a fairly high standard of living; there are probably poor people, but I saw no beggars. Bhutan produces beautiful handicrafts, especially in silk and weaving, and some of the religious art compares well with Tibet's finest. My stay in Bhutan reminded me that the whole of the Himalayas shows strong Tibetan cultural influence, chiefly linked to the Kagyu and Nyingma schools.

Rinpoche offered Bhutan's king a set of the *Nyingma Edition of the Tibetan Buddhist Canon*. He also visited thirty-two monasteries and holy places, making offerings and giving funds. Places visited included the following:

Khyentse Rinpoche's monastery

Paro Kudung Chorten,
the stupa of Tangtong Gyalpo

Namkhai Gonpa, the major
Kagyu monastery, Thimphu

Tarpa Ling, the main monastery
of Longchenpa

Thendul gyi Lakang
at Paro Kyerchu

Taksang Monastery in Bhutan, associated with Padmasambhava. It burned to the ground in 1998, but is now being rebuilt.

Sekar Gutog	Jamchen Lakang
Memay Lamay Gonpa	Mewar Tso
Drubtob Rinpoche Gonpa	Lhachem Pemasar Trungkhyim
Gengteng Gonpa	Jampal Lakang
Purna Shapo Drang	Lalung Gonpa
Nyima Lung Gonpa	Paro Taksang
Kurje Lakang, Bumtang	Thimpu Dudul Chorten

Based on that auspicious beginning, TNMC has continued to support Dharma activity in Bhutan, and TAP has been able to join in these efforts. In recent years, Her Majesty the Queen Mother Kelsang Wangchuk has followed suggestions from Tarthang Tulku in sponsoring the restoration of holy places in Bhutan and in supporting the continuity of traditional practices.

Rinpoche has placed special emphasis on four sites in Bhutan regarded as sacred to Padmasambhava: Bumtang Kurje Lhakang, Paro Taksang, Kyerchu Jowo Lhakang, and Senge Dzong. He has also encouraged Bhutanese lamas and the Queen Mother to support the rebuilding of Tharpa Ling, the central monastery of Longchenpa in Bhutan, as well as other retreat sites linked to this great Nyingma master. In addition, he has donated funds toward the construction of a retreat center at Sengay Dzong under the direction of Lama Serpo, holder of the Nyingtig lineage transmitted by Adzom Drugpa.

In the spring of 1998, a great tragedy befell Bhutan when Taksang Monastery, one of the four "Tiger's Tail" monasteries established in locations where Guru Padmasambhava meditated in the eighth century, burned to the ground. Both TNMC and TAP have dedicated funds to its rebuilding, now underway.

RENEWING TAP'S MANDATE

TAP's decision in 1988 to take substantial responsibility for the new Nyingma Shedra in Nepal meant that it had to become more active at every level. An administrative structure was put in place in which two directors shared responsibility for TAP's activities, with a special focus on fundraising. As described in Chapter Four, the Pen Friend Program was reactivated, and the directors initiated a review of the business aspects of TAP's operations, making sure its bookkeeping procedures, data bases, banking, budgeting, and management were running smoothly and had the capacity to expand.

Fundraising initiatives that were initiated at this time included seminars in Los Angeles on the practice of Kum Nye, a Tibetan mind-body discipline introduced to the West by Tarthang Tulku and taught with great success at the Nyingma Institute and other Nyingma centers. In addition, TAP received three modest grants from foundations to carry on with its work.

With all these initiatives, a spirit of growth and energy began to manifest in all of TAP's operations. This dynamic was fostered when TAP moved into new offices in a building in west Berkeley considered an historical landmark. Given the name "Dharma House," the new facilities, which expanded into an adjoining warehouse a few years later, housed all of the business operations of Dharma Publishing and a portion of the production facilities for the Yeshe De Project, a text preservation initiative that was becoming increasingly active.

The new facilities made it possible for TAP to reach out to the public in more effective ways. Soon several work-study students (who took classes and programs at the Nyingma Institute at night and on the weekends and worked

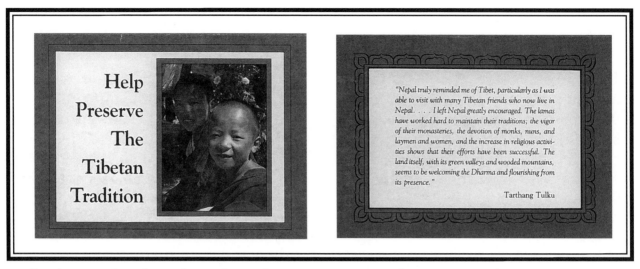

A fundraising brochure from the early 1990s announced new TAP and TNMC initiatives.

for Nyingma organizations during the day) were offering their energy and skills to TAP's growing list of projects. These included furnishing and staffing the offices at Dharma House, planning and organizing large mailings and a variety of consciousness-raising projects, the promotion of TAP at fairs and book shows, the creation of greeting cards and other items with Tibetan themes, and the installation of a new database for pen friends and donors.

Direct mailings now became an increasingly important element in TAP's strategy for fundraising. Brochures and other mailings served a dual purpose, encouraging contributions on the one hand and educating the public about the plight of Tibetan refugees on the other. Initial mailings in 1989 promoted the revived Pen Friend Program, solicited general donations, and aimed at increasing awareness of TAP's work. In 1990, TAP developed and printed new fundraising materials and mailed over 20,000 brochures. In 1992, TAP sent out over 35,000 pieces of mail, far surpassing previous efforts.

Late in 1993, TAP printed 200,000 copies of a new brochure intended for distribution over the next several years For the first time, it now began purchasing mailing lists from other organizations. Although this added expense marked a departure from TAP's long-standing commitment to keep its administrative costs and overhead to an absolute minimum, the results were very positive. By the end of 1993, TAP had over 1,800 donors and supporters in its database, many of whom were regular contributors. In countries on three continents, individuals who had been touched by Tibetan Buddhism or by the Tibetan people and their culture now had an opportunity to express their support by contributing to the vital task of preserving a great heritage.

Through such support, TAP was able to move to a new level of effectiveness. In the six years from 1988 to 1993, TAP generated more than $398,000 in donations and other forms of income—more than three times the sum that TAP had received in the fourteen years from 1974 to 1987.

SUPPORT FOR ART AND LEARNING

As the monasteries of the refugee communities become more firmly established in the 1970s and 1980s, a few of the leading lamas were able to found shedras (institutions of higher learning). With TAP now actively involved in raising funds, it was able to join TNMC in offering financial support for building or maintaining five shedras:

Namdroling, founded in Bylakuppe by H.H. Penor Rinpoche. Offerings made by the two organizations included food, clothing, medicine, and stipends for 250 lamas for three years.

Ven. Dechen Dorje's shedra in Sikkim.

Ven. Rigo Tulku's shedra in Bir

Nyingmapa Lamas College, Dehra Dun

Shedra of H.E. Taklung Tsetrul, Simla.

Over the sixy years from 1988–1993, the Pen Friend program made disbursements in support of these five shedras as follows:

Sikkim Shedra	$6,020
Rigo Tulku, Bir	8,500
Khochen Tulku, Dehra Dun	6,800
Taklung Tsetrul, Simla	3,620

A total of $3,120 also went to Ka-Nying Shedrup Ling and Nagi Gonpa in Nepal, two centers maintained by the learned master Urgyen Tulku. Another $7,800 was distributed to independent centers and lamas.

An opportunity for TAP to support the arts of Tibet came in 1994, when it received a request for assistance from the Gesar Dance Troupe. King Gesar is considered by Tibetans to be an incarnation of Guru Padmasambhava, and the Gesar epic helps define the Tibetan character, much as the legend of King Arthur helps define what it means to be British. Traditionally, Tibetans would journey many days to watch dances based on the Gesar story, performed by troupes consisting of as many as three hundred monks. During the diaspora, only one dancer managed to escape to India. At the request of H.H. Dudjom Rinpoche, she began to revive the Gesar dances. Over the course of several years, TAP was able to provide the Dance Troupe with funds to purchase the elaborate costumes required as well as food and other basic necessities.

TAP PUBLICATIONS

TAP's involvement with publications had its start in the 1970s, when it helped sponsor production of the first books in the Jataka Tales Series. In 1988, as TAP began to expand, Dharma Publishing developed a new set of six Jataka Tales, beautifully illustrated and printed in full color with gold line-art. As with previous Jatakas (and those that followed), TAP received royalties on their sale. Although the amounts were not large, they helped TAP cover administrative costs at a time of rapid growth. In 1990, TAP entered into a similar arrangement with Amber Lotus, a publisher of greeting cards and related products that had originated as a project of Dharma Publishing. Amber Lotus produced a set of Tibetan Image greeting cards, which portrayed landscapes and mountains

and striking images of Tibetan lay people. A portion of proceeds went to TAP, where they helped cover TAP's administrative costs and overhead.

An important step in presenting the history and culture of Tibet came in 1986, with the publication of *Ancient Tibet*, produced by the Yeshe De Buddhist Research and Translation Project. The purpose of the book, as set forth by Tarthang Tulku in its preface, matched closely the mission pursued by TAP: "In the last few decades, Tibet has undergone dramatic, even drastic changes. My hope is that this volume will encourage the understanding of the value of the traditional culture while it still remains, and remind Tibetans of their ancient heritage."

A blend of historical research and scientific data, *Ancient Tibet* offered information on the geography and geology of Tibet and an overview of its prehistory, as revealed both by archaeological investigation and in accounts preserved by Tibetan historians. Written in clear, non-technical language, it opened new areas of inquiry to a larger audience, including the Tibetan refugees themselves. Tibetans studying this presentation could learn how their traditions linked up to discoveries of modern geology and archaeology, as well as to the historical records of early Tibet, China, and the ancient kingdoms of Central Asia. This comprehensive perspective encouraged appreciation for traditional Tibetan accounts that might otherwise have been dismissed as myth.

The success of *Ancient Tibet*, which won praise from scholars and Dharma students alike, led TAP to start on a new project: a work on the Tibetan diaspora and the efforts of Tibetans in exile to renew the foundations of their tradition. Published early in 1992 under the title *From the Roof of the World: Refugees of Tibet*, this new book was conceived as an illustrated record that would serve to document the work of the Tibetan Aid Project, while also communicating the saga of a people's struggle for cultural survival in a world turned upside down.

Intended to offer an accurate historical and visual record, *From the Roof of the World* drew heavily on pictures and documents received by TAP from centers and individuals as they faced the challenges of making a new home for Tibetan civilization. Rinpoche gave TAP

A general overview of history reveals that the continuity and integrity of an ancient civilization can persist despite changing circumstances. But history also shows that a heritage can be lost, if people relinquish knowledge of the past. . . . In previous centuries, the slower rhythm of change supported the continuity of older ways in the face of new circumstances, and also provided more time for new ideas to grow naturally. But in today's world, rapid change affects all aspects of life. . . .

Confronted with the variety of lifestyles and philosophies available in the modern world, younger generations who no longer identify with their own heritage have little basis for their choices. If we abandon our knowledge of the past, then the human heritage will gradually slip from memory all over the world—and with it a precious reservoir of wisdom that belongs to all people. The fuller our knowledge of the past, the more likely we are to guide the future with intelligence, without repeating old mistakes.

In these times, it seems especially important to know the past, not only to study its lessons, but also to preserve its knowledge. Faced with the complex difficulties of modern times, we cannot afford to discard such a rich heritage. If the wisdom and experience of older civilizations were joined to the store of modern expertise, the fully mature body of humanity's knowledge could become the foundation for world harmony.

Tarthang Tulku, *Ancient Tibet*

photos taken twenty years earlier that documented the earliest days of the diaspora, some of which appear in earlier chapters of this book. Dharma Publishing editors drew on their own continuing research to write a sixty-page introduction on the land and people of Tibet and the history of Dharma transmission. For its part in the production of the book, TAP provided records and photographs, and worked closely with the editors for the portions that presented the story of TAP's efforts under the guidance of TNMC. A special feature of *Roof of the World* was an important series of maps portraying the physical landscape of Tibet and locating major sites that were literally being erased from Chinese cartography, and thus from the minds of a new generation of Tibetans, growing up without access to their own traditions.

Once again, Tarthang Tulku conveyed in just a few words the vision that guided publication of the book:

Over the years, Tibetan refugees in India and Nepal have sent me many photographs of their activities, including ceremonies we have sponsored. These photographs, together with the snapshots Tibetans seeking pen friends have sent to TAP, provide the heart of the book.

From the Roof of the World

Refugees of Tibet

Our primary purpose in preparing this book is to offer these images to the refugees themselves, that they may more fully understand and appreciate the value of the experiences recorded here. In keeping with the policies that TAP and TNMC have followed since the earliest days, TAP will use proceeds from the sale of the book solely to benefit the Tibetan refugees.

The photographs in *From the Roof of the World* document one of the most significant cultural migrations of modern times. The early scenes of deep suffering and disorientation are followed by chapters that chronicle early stages of accomplishment and make clear the promise of the future. Revealing both the anguish and the determination of a people in distress, *From the Roof of the World* serves as a gesture toward preserving a legacy of cultural pride and achievement, one that future generations will be able to study and appreciate.

FOUNDING INTERNATIONAL OPERATIONS

In mid-1990, Tarthang Tulku asked TAP's directors to establish TAP offices in the four international Nyingma centers, located in Germany, Holland, and Brazil. Officers of these centers, many of whom already had connections to TAP's activities, welcomed enthusiastically the opportunity to promote TAP's projects, and the Pen Friend program met with a warm response from their students and supporters. In 1994, TAP added another center in Gifu, Japan. Both Nyingma Centrum Nederland and Nyingma Zentrum Deutschland have now incorporated their Tibetan Aid Project branches as independent nonprofit organizations.

Within a few years of their founding, TAP's international offices were collecting significant amounts for the support of monastic centers and shedras and the monks who practiced and studied there. At the German and Dutch centers, funds were raised specifically for the support of nuns. In 1992, a representative from the Berkeley TAP office traveled to Holland and Germany to discuss TAP's goals and vision with the TAP administrators at both centers. During this visit, basic procedures were introduced at each center to ensure that they followed the same careful rules regarding distribution of funds adopted by TAP in America.

By 1993, contributions to TAP from the international centers had expanded dramatically, to over $20,000 per year. Although these contributions and the scale of the activities at the international offices diminished in later years, an effort is currently underway to revitalize TAP's activity on a global scale. Plans include establishing a TAP presence in Great Britain, where one of TAP's directors has already had considerable success with fundraising.

STEADY FINANCIAL GROWTH

The guidelines instituted by Rinpoche when the Tibetan Nyingma Relief Foundation was established in 1974 required that all donations go directly to the purposes intended by their donors, with overhead costs kept to a bare minimum. The expanding scope of TAP's activities after 1988 made it necessary to reconsider this directive in light of the added expenses associated with bulk mailing and other promotional activity required to increase the flow of donations. The following year by year synopsis of TAP's fundraising efforts in relation to its costs from 1988 to 1993 reveals how rapidly TAP's situation was changing and clarifies the need to modify certain aspects of its operations.

1988

During the 1988 fiscal year, TAP's total income was $12,431. Only about $500 came in donations. The bulk of the funds was provided by TNMC, which transferred $5,500 to TAP to sponsor ceremonies at specified monasteries, and by Dharma Publishing, whose roy-

alty payments came to over $6,400 (representing a partial payment on Jataka Tale royalties that had not been made in many years). Overhead expenses were just over $200.

1989

During the 1989 fiscal year, TAP's income more than doubled, to $25,963. This included a $5,000 transfer from TNMC to sponsor ceremonies at monasteries, as well as Dharma Publishing royalty payments of $5,000. Donations increased to $8,683. In addition, a jewelry business founded by a TAP director had now gone into operation, and was able to donate to TAP a net of $765 from its first year in operation; Kum Nye seminars in Los Angeles generated another $1,515. For the first time in many years, TAP received a foundation grant: $5,000 from the Kongsgaard Foundation. The Pen Friend Program was once more in operation, and TAP's expanded staff was actively involved in fundraising efforts, including the creation of a set of Tibetan Image greeting cards. Overhead expenses were $796.

1990

In the 1990 fiscal year, TAP's income almost tripled, to a total of $76,104. Of this amount, $66,082 came from donations, including a single gift of $25,500 —the largest in TAP's history up to that point. With the Pen Friend Program in full operation, income from Pen Friend donations were $25,800. Other sources of income included a rummage sale that generated $2,470, donations from the jewelry business of $6,399, and income from three Los Angeles Kum Nye seminars totaling $1,152. Tibetan Image greeting card sales and sales from a new project—incense from the Nyingma Institute of Nepal—also generated a modest level of funds.

Corresponding to this dramatic rise in income was an increase in overhead expenses, which totaled $8,207: almost 11% of total income. Most of this cost was linked directly to fundraising efforts. TAP mailed more than 20,000 pieces during the year, resulting in mailing costs of $3,286. Other costs included $856 for office support, $2,173 for printing, and $1,355 for postage, bank fees, and other expenses.

In keeping with TAP guidelines, none of these administrative costs were met out of general donations. Instead, they came out of Dharma Publishing royalties paid in the previous two years and donations specifically earmarked for overhead costs by the donor.

1991

The 1991 fiscal year did not meet with the same success as in 1990. TAP's total income dropped back to $35,608, an amount that included $12,000 transferred from TNMC for ceremonies. Just over $16,000 came from donations, and $4,670 came from contributions generated through jewelry sales. Los Angeles Kum Nye seminars brought in $600, while Tibetan Image greeting card sales generated $2,157 and incense sales $160.

Overhead expenses came to $5,784, or 16% of revenues. This amount was somewhat inflated by the purchase of TAP's first computer. Other significant expenses included phone bills of $1,150, public relations expenses of $952, and printing costs of $774. The remaining costs went for such expenses as bank charges, bulk mail, travel, office supplies and support, and postage.

Throughout 1991, TAP continued to experiment with new ways of reaching the public. A new brochure was designed and a card depicting the Bodh Gaya Stupa was printed to be used as a gift to donors acknowledging their contributions. A set of postcards was also created, and small advertisements were placed in the Oakland Tribune.

1992

In the 1992 fiscal year, TAP sent out a total of 35,000 pieces of mail. As a direct result, total income increased substantially, to $133,794. Of this amount, $126,384 came from donations, including one large contribution of $6,400. Donations to the Pen Friend Program, amounting to $40,206, constituted less than one-third of the total. Dharma Publishing paid TAP $4,583 in Jataka Tales royalties, and sales of *From the Roof of the World*, TAP's newly published account of the Tibetan refugees, brought in $1,299. Incense sales generated $1,195, and miscellaneous projects accounted for $332.

Overhead expenditures for the year totaled $14,926, or 11 percent of income. The major expenses included $4,211 for mailing, costs for incense of $2,257, printing costs of $2,586, $686 in postage, $818 in phone bills, and expenses for office supplies and support of $3,935. All overhead expenses were covered by Jataka royalties and income contributed by the jewelry business in previous years.

1993

Income in 1993 was $112,237, suggesting that TAP had begun to stabilize at a new level of effectiveness. Donations, however dropped to $76,553. Mailings had now proved their effectiveness in generating donations, even if the associated costs stretched TAP's financial guidelines. A second grant came from the Kongsgaard Foundation for $5,000, and TNMC transferred $11,020 toward ceremonies. Donations from the jewelry business came to $7,927, and $10,500 came in from in Jataka royalties. Book and jewelry sales in the Netherlands generated $1,191.

With reduced mailing costs, operational and overhead expenses for 1993 came to $9,946, or less than 9% of income. Major expenses included $1,358 for bulk mailings, $1,222 for public relations expenses, $1,600 for promotion, $1,630 for office supplies and expenses, $1,126 for phone bills, $710 for printing, $512 for fund raising events, $406 for incense, and $1,381 for bank fees, printing, transportation, fees, advertising, and other costs.

The pattern of income and expenses during these years revealed a strong current of support in the public at large for TAP's goal of preserving Tibetan culture. At the same time, the growth of interest in Tibetan Buddhism had a paradoxical effect. Individuals sympathetic to the Tibetan cause now regularly came in contact with a wide variety of organizations actively seeking funds for the Tibetan people, all with their own perspective and goals. With its unique emphasis on preserving the whole of the Tibetan heritage for future generations and for the sake of all humanity, TAP had to make a concerted effort to communicate clearly the value of its projects and convey the special urgency of its mission.

PART FOUR

BUILDING THE FUTURE

CHAPTER SEVEN

THE WORLD PEACE CEREMONIES

A new focus of activity for TAP emerged in the early 1990s. It began with the World Peace Ceremonies, first held at Bodh Gaya, India in 1989. Organized and sponsored by Tarthang Tulku and TNMC, the ceremonies became an annual event and a focal point for the distribution of books and art to thousands of Tibetans who assembled from all parts of Asia to participate. In response to the opportunity the World Peace Ceremonies presented, TAP reshaped its vision of how best to achieve its goal: contributing to the preservation of Tibetan culture and the wisdom of the Tibetan tradition.

ORIGINS OF THE WORLD PEACE CEREMONY

Of all the holy places in Buddhism, none is more vital than Bodh Gaya, site of the Vajrasana, the unshakeable seat where the Buddha attained enlightenment. According to the Tibetan tradition, Bodh Gaya is a place of special power and blessings, unique in all the earth: the place where all the Buddhas of our age, past, present, and future, attain enlightenment.

Through the centuries, great masters traveled to Bodh Gaya to study and practice. Here, at the center of the Buddhist world, their prayers and their focused meditation evoked the blessings of enlightenment, magnifying the power of this sacred site and enabling its blessings to flow outward to all beings.

Abandoned and nearly forgotten for some seven centuries after the great Buddhist institutions of India were pillaged and destroyed, Bodh Gaya was rediscovered and partially restored in the late nineteenth century. Buddhists of many lands contributed to this effort, together with archaeologists fascinated by Bodh Gaya as a place that had inspired thousands with awe and reverence through the centuries.

By the time of the Tibetan diaspora, Bodh Gaya was again available for practice and pilgrimage. Restoration efforts had preserved the Mahabodhi, the great stupa-crowned temple erected on the site where the Buddha had attained enlightenment. At its side the Bodhi Tree still flourished, the direct descendant of the tree that sheltered the meditating Buddha on the night of

Opposite: The assembly of monks at the annual World Peace Ceremony in Bodh Gaya, India. The wrapped bundles are books, prepared by the Nyingma centers and shipped by TAP.

his Awakening. Pilgrims were once again able to offer their prayers at the very place where the Buddha resolved to make the Dharma available for the welfare of all sentient beings.

In Volume Five of the *Annals of the Nyingma Lineage in America*, Tarthang Tulku described his own introduction to the Vajrasana, his resolve to restore its importance for Tibetan Buddhists and for Buddhists around the world, and his first steps toward accomplishing this goal:

My teacher Lord Jamyang Khyentse Chokyi Lodro had made repeated pilgrimages to Bodh Gaya to pray and offer butter lamps at the Maha-bodhi Temple. After his death in 1959, out of respect for my teacher's great kindness and deep concern for the suffering of my people and the destruction of the Dharma in Tibet, I made a pilgrimage to this holy place. I felt the long history of Bodh Gaya (known in Tibet as Vajrasana, or Dorje Den) like a living presence.

I prayed strongly, wishing that the Dharma could come alive again through the power of the merit and virtue of such great masters, to bring peace to the world and relieve the sufferings of sentient beings. Twice, when I prayed openly from the heart, I received answers. I felt deep appreciation for my teacher, who came here to pray at a time when such a pilgrimage was rare and there were no resources available for traditional offerings. I still believe that his devotion and prayers helped sustain the

Tibetan Dharma through these painful years.

Later I studied Bodh Gaya's long association with the Nyingma lineage, tracing from the time of the Vidyadharas. . . . The Buddha, the Arhats, Bodhisattvas, great siddhas, Dzogchen masters, Tibetan lotsawas—so many enlightened masters had consecrated this holy place with their prayers that simply being here seemed to have merit in itself. Invoking the blessings of these masters here, at the most spiritually charged place on earth, is like entering an invisible temple that their practice has imprinted in space: The power of prayer becomes enormous.

When this holy place fell into disrepair, the world went out of balance. I wished to help remedy this situation. In the late 1970s, I began sponsoring prayers at Bodh Gaya and other locations. Funds for these ceremonies were provided by TNMC, while direct support for monasteries was largely generated through the Tibetan Aid Project. In 1978, H.H. Dilgo Khyentse Rinpoche granted my request for a ceremony: Under TNMC's sponsorship, he convened an assembly at Bodh Gaya to offer a hundred thousand recitations of the Bhadracharya Pranidhana Raja, a powerful prayer to realize enlightenment for the benefit of all beings.

In 1981, I requested His Holiness to lead one hundred thousand recitations of the Manjushri Namasamgiti at Bodh Gaya. Unable to attend, His Holiness transferred the funds

> ### THE IMPORTANCE OF PILGRIMAGE
>
> " 'Here the Tathagata was born!' This, Ananda, is a place that a pious person should visit and look upon with feelings of reverence.
>
> " 'Here the Tathagata became fully enlightened in unsurpassed, supreme Enlightenment!' This, Ananda, is a place that a pious person should visit and look upon with feelings of reverence.
>
> " 'Here the Tathagata set rolling the unexcelled Wheel of the Dharma!' This, Ananda, is a place that a pious person should visit and look upon with feelings of reverence.
>
> " 'Here the Tathagata passed away into the state of Nirvana in which no element of clinging remains!' This, Ananda, is a place that a pious person should visit and look upon with feelings of reverence.
>
> "These, Ananda, are the four places that a pious person should visit and look upon with feelings of reverence. And truly there will come to these places, Ananda, pious monks and nuns, laymen and laywomen, reflecting: 'Here the Tathagata was born! Here the Tathagata became fully enlightened in unsurpassed, supreme Enlightenment! Here the Tathagata set rolling the unexcelled Wheel of the Dharma! Here the Tathagata passed away into the state of Nirvana in which no element of clinging remains.'
>
> "And whoever, Ananda, should die on such a pilgrimage with his heart established in faith, at the breaking up of the body, after death: He will be reborn in a realm of heavenly happiness."
>
> Mahaparinibbana-sutta

that TNMC had donated for the ceremony to Ven. Dodrup Chen Rinpoche, and he and Khenpo Dechen Dorje performed the ceremony together with their students.

During the 1980s, Rinpoche made several other attempts to sponsor ceremonies at Bodh Gaya, but his lama friends had many responsibilities, and it was not easy for them to arrange for such gatherings. Finally he decided on a more direct course of action. In 1989 he wrote to his friends and fellow lamas in the Nyingma lineage, inviting them to join him at the Mahabodhi Temple in Bodh Gaya for several weeks of prayers dedicated to world peace. In December of that year, he returned to India for the first time in more than twenty years. He prepared the site and made the countless arrangements required. When the prayers began, he helped conduct the daily ceremonies.

Rinpoche wrote of this occasion in an article in *Gesar*:

My initial impulse in founding the Monlam Chenmo was to follow the example of my teacher. I also saw this as a way to honor our parents, families, and friends who suffered so greatly or lost their lives in the great tragedy of our people. Then, too, I felt that Buddhism should have its own most holy place of pilgrimage, and wanted to encourage the practice of pilgrimage to holy places. Most of all, I was inspired by the urgent need to restore peace and harmony in these troubled times. I believed that if we joined together to pray with deep devotion to the Three Jewels, accumulating merit and wisdom, we could become the agents of the Enlightened Lineage. Then the power of our efforts would be inconceivably magnified.

Over a period of twenty-five days, seven hundred tulkus, lamas, monks, and nuns offered three hundred thousand recitations of the Manjushri Namasamgiti. This marked the first time in history that monks and lamas from so many Nyingma monasteries, representing all the lineages and traditions, had come together in a major convocation, which was especially significant in light of their separation from their home monasteries in Tibet. To extend the blessings further, TNMC also sponsored a hundred thousand recitations of the Manjushri Namasamgiti at five Gelug monasteries.

When the ceremonies ended in January, the assembly requested Tarthang Tulku to organize similar ceremonies at Bodh Gaya for the following year. The second ceremonies, held in January 1991, were attended by 1,500 participants. They started on precisely the same day that hostilities broke out in a major conflict in the Middle East, making more evident than ever the importance of prayers for world peace.

At the end of that second ceremony, participants requested that the ceremonies become an annual event. In earlier times, when Tibet was still an independent land, the Monlam Chenmo, or Great Prayer Ceremony, had been held annually in Lhasa. Rinpoche and his friends decided that the Monlams could be adapted to the conditions of the exile community and the pressing need in all parts of the world for inner peace and for peace among groups and nations. Since then, the Ngagyur Nyingma Monlam Chenmo, organized as a ten-day ceremony, has been held in Bodh Gaya each year.

A NEW TRADITION OF PRAYER AT THE CENTER OF THE BUDDHIST WORLD

The third World Peace Ceremony in 1992 was attended by two thousand participants, and the fourth, in 1993, by 3,700 tulkus, abbots, lamas, monks, yogins, and nuns, as well as 2,500 lay people. Ten thousand lamas, monks, nuns, and lay people came to the ceremony in 1994. From 1995 onward between five thousand and seven thousand abbots, lamas, yogins, monks, and nuns attended each year, together with many thousands of lay people. Participants traveled to Bodh Gaya from more than three hundred monasteries and centers located in India, Nepal, Tibet, Bhutan, and throughout the Himalayas. From 1989 through 1996, Rinpoche himself attended the Monlam Chenmo each year, with the exception of the second ceremony, held in 1991.

Reviewing these auspicious circumstances in 1997, Tarthang Tulku wrote:

The World Peace Ceremonies have gone far toward revitalizing the ancient holy places. Bodh Gaya in particular has been transformed in recent years into a living beacon of enlightenment. Here Tibetans who have lost their homelands have found a fresh focus for their prayers and devotion, and their devotion has breathed new life into this most holy place.

The ceremonies have substantially increased the flow of alms to beggars in Bihar, India's most impoverished state. Business has improved, invigorating the surrounding community. The ceremonies have helped focus international attention on the area, increasing its status within India itself. Here Western students have been able to participate with the Sangha in traditional practices and experience for themselves the power of devotion offered at places empowered by the actions of the Lord Buddha.

The beings of the six realms are in great pain, sinking into the turbulent waters of samsara. If we wish to help, there is no more meritorious action than to participate in the
Monlam Chenmo. When we pray at Dorje Den, the seat of the Buddha's enlightenment, we are really meditating on the teaching that we can all obtain perfect enlightenment. By communicating with the power that radiates through this sacred place, we sow the seeds for the enlightenment of all beings and the peace and happiness of the entire world. Anyone with faith in the Dharma knows that when abbots of the great monasteries, enlightened lineage holders, yogins, monks and nuns, lay people, and Westerners assemble to express their devotions, the world will experience the blessings directly. If we pray with true compassion, we may help counteract the forces of evil and confusion. And if our faith is strong, we will meet our responsibility to assure that the Dharma continues to manifest, now and in times to come.

When the power of the Vajrasana opens, we enter the enlightened mandala. Surely this will help us find the inspiration to continue the work of the enlightened masters who preceded us.

TNMC sponsored, organized, and managed the World Peace Ceremonies until 1993. In that year, Rinpoche established the Nyingma Monlam Chenmo International Foundation, in cooperation with H.H. Penor Rinpoche and other prominent Nyingma leaders. Starting with the ceremony in 1994, Nyingma lamas in Asia have worked through the Monlam Chenmo Foundation to share responsibility for administration and coordination of the

Above: Lamas, monks, yogins, and lay people walk where the Buddha walked. Below: The assembly of monks gathered around the Mahabodhi Temple and Bodhi Tree. Each year the assembly renews its dedication to the Three Jewels and its commitment to serve all beings.

High lamas of the Nyingma Sangha assemble at Bodh Gaya in 1993. Here at the Fourth World Peace Ceremony, Tarthang Tulku announced creation of the Monlam Chenmo Foundation, intended to fund the ceremonies in perpetuity.

OFFERING MANDALA FOR THE WORLD PEACE CEREMONY

Because we and all beings live in dark times, we offer the light of thousands of lamps and candles.

Because we and all beings live in dull discouragement, we offer the uplifting beauty of flowers, the mysterious fragrance of incense, and the transporting melodies of the chant.

Because we and all beings live in conflict, we offer the harmony of the Sangha, seated together on the four sides of the Enlightenment Stupa.

With this mandala offering, we ask that the healing energy of the Dharma rain down upon us now and in all lifetimes to come.

Tarthang Tulku (Gesar XII: 2)

annual Monlam Chenmo. That same year Rinpoche founded the Bodh Gaya Religious Trust, a non-profit entity under the laws of the United States whose funds are dedicated entirely to continuation of the annual Monlam Chenmo.

MONLAMS AT HOLY SITES FOR ALL THE FOUR SCHOOLS

The success of the World Peace Ceremonies in Bodh Gaya encouraged Rinpoche to seek other opportunities for uniting the Sangha in prayer. In 1995, he established the Longchenpa Monlam Ceremony at the Damekh Stupa in Sarnath, where the Buddha first taught the Dharma. Held in honor of the parinirvana of the great fourteenth-century Nyingma master Longchenpa, these ceremonies marked the renewal of a tradition observed for centuries in many Nyingma monasteries. Occurring just a few days after the close of the Monlam Chenmo, the Longchenpa Monlam has been held each year since. Rinpoche has established the Varna Longchen Foundation to provide for its continuation in perpetuity.

The World Peace Ceremonies in Bodh Gaya and the Longchenpa Sadhana in Sarnath are both organized on behalf of the Nyingma school. However, Tarthang Tulku has always emphasized the importance of preserving the distinct identity of all the major schools of Tibetan Buddhism and acknowledging the contributions each has made to Tibetan culture and to the Buddhist heritage. Once the Nyingma Monlam Chenmo was well established and its benefits clear, he approached lamas from the Sarma

traditions with a proposal for organizing annual Monlams at the three other great pilgrimage sites of Buddhism in India: Lumbini (where the Buddha was born), Sarnath, and Kushinagara (where he passed away). The proposal met with a warm response. In 1993 and again in 1994, TNMC sponsored Monlams for both the Sakya and Kagyu schools in Lumbini and a Monlam for the Gelug school at Sarnath. Due to logistical problems, it has not been possible to organize similar ceremonies at Kushinagara.

When the first ceremonies proved successful, Tarthang Tulku encouraged each school to establish foundations for their continuation. The Sakya Foundation was headed by H.H. Sakya Trizin, the Kagyu Foundation by Ven. Chokyi Nyima Rinpoche, and the Gelugpa Foundation by Ven. Samdhong Rinpoche. TNMC offered a hundred thousand dollars in seed money to each foundation. H.H. Sakya Trizin and H.E. Chogyal Trichen have organized and conducted ceremonies for the Sakya school each year since 1993, and H.H. Sakya Trizin has taken these opportunities to give major teachings. H.E. Choling Rinpoche and Ven. Tulku Chokyi Nyima have organized the ceremonies for the Kagyu school, and Ven. Samdhong Rinpoche and his committee made the arrangements for the initial ceremonies for the Gelug school.

Despite some obstacles, including the apparent loss of funds originally contributed for the Gelugpa Monlam that had to be replaced, the ceremonies have been a success. They appear to have greatly strengthened the Sanghas of all four schools.

Opposite: Candles and butter lamps at Bodh Gaya, lit to dispel the darkness of ignorance.

PRAYER FOR ALL BEINGS

Beyond the beliefs of any one religion,
there is the truth of the human spirit.
Beyond the power of the nations, there is the power
of the human heart. Beyond the ordinary mind,
the power of wisdom, love and healing energy
are at work in the universe. When we can find
peace within our hearts, we contact
these universal powers.
This is our only hope.

Tarthang Tulku
(World Peace Ceremony 1991)

TNMC has also sponsored Monlams on special occasions. On February 5, 1994, and again on March 17, 1995, TNMC sponsored one-day ceremonies for world peace at the Bodhnath Stupa in Boudha, near Kathmandu, inviting representatives of all four schools to participate. More than four thousand monks, lamas, and nuns assembled for the ceremony in 1994 and five hundred for the ceremony in 1995. The following year, TNMC sponsored a memorial ceremony at the same site in honor of Urgyen Tulku, a widely respected Nyingma master and abbot who passed away early in 1996 after a lifetime of service to the Dharma. The ceremony was attended by seven tulkus, ten khenpos, 1,862 monks, lamas, and nuns, and thousands of lay people.

The ceremonies initiated by TNMC in Bodh Gaya met with an especially warm response in the Buddhist kingdom of Bhutan, to the north of India. Each year monks and lay people (more than ten thousand in some years), traveled from Bhutan to Bodh Gaya to participate in the Ceremony. In the early mornings, the lay people circumambulated the Mahabodhi Temple, and during the day they took up places on the edge of the assembly. In 1994, TNMC sponsored a Monlam ceremony in Bhutan, inspiring the Bhutanese to organize their own annual Monlam Ceremony. It is directed by the World Peace Monlam Tshokpa of Bhutan.

TAP'S PARTICIPATION IN THE MONLAM CHENMOS

The Monlam Chenmo ceremonies fit perfectly with TAP's mission of preserving Tibetan culture and encouraging the strength and stability of the Tibetan exile community. For the first ceremony in 1989, TAP contributed over a thousand

The Sangha of the four schools gathers at Bodhnath Stupa in Kathmandu.

dollars to create book covers for texts to be donated to participants, a hint of the role that TAP would come to play in later years. For the second ceremony, held in 1991, TAP contributed $36,000 for the modest daily offerings made to participants that covered their basic needs and helped defray their travel expenses. It also donated $3,690 toward the creation of large banners that were mounted on the four sides of the Mahabodhi Temple, $300 for daily offerings at the temple, and $500 for miscellaneous travel expenses.

In later years, as the quantity of books and art being sent increased dramatically, TAP shifted its focus of support to funding the shipping and distribution of texts and sacred images. However, it also continued to make modest financial donations in support of TNMC's sponsorship of the Monlam Chenmo.

TAP also contributed regularly to the Monlams of the Sarma schools, which began in 1993. In 1992, TAP donated five thousand dollars to the Sakya Monlam planned for Lumbini, using money given to it by TNMC for this specific purpose. Eventually, after making small donations to the annual Monlams of all four schools for several years, TAP adopted the policy of making a more substantial donation to at least one of the Monlams each year.

In the past decade, the World Peace Ceremonies have served as a natural focus for TAP's fundraising activities. Deeply moving videotapes of the annual ceremonies have enabled TAP to convey to friends and interested individuals the role that the Dharma and the monastic traditions play in the lives of the Tibetan people.

The ceremonies have also served as an inspiration for TAP's staff, donors, volunteers, and friends, both in the United States and abroad. Over the years, many individuals with links to the work of the Tibetan Aid Project have had the opportunity to attend the Monlam Chenmo and to participate in the distribution of books and art. Having seen for themselves the reverence that all Tibetans—whether monks and nuns or lay people—have for the tradition, TAP workers and friends have returned with a deep conviction in the significance of TAP's work. Observing the lamas, monks, and nuns gathered in prayer, listening to the chants and sensing the deep devotion of the lay participants, those who attend can glimpse the deeper meaning of what is happening at the ceremonies. Inevitably their experience leaves them with a better understanding of the merit and purpose of the efforts that TAP's supporters and staff have made through the years.

Soon after the Ceremonies had been inaugurated, TAP found a way to express this connection in a very personal way. Each year TAP donors and friends prepare prayers expressing their own deepest wishes, and a TAP representative reads them at the Mahabodhi Temple while the ceremony is in progress. The names of all of TAP's donors are then read aloud, followed by special prayers for their well-being. In this way, the blessings of the ceremonies touch everyone who has supported TAP's work, whether through donations or through direct participation in its activities.

SHIPPING TEXTS AND SACRED ART

THIRTY YEARS OF PRESERVATION

Starting from his earliest years in exile, Tarthang Tulku worked to preserve and distribute Tibetan texts. As described in Chapter Three, Dharma Mudranalaya, the publishing company he founded in India, overcame serious obstacles to produce more than twenty texts. Founded anew in America, Dharma Publishing produced the *Nyingma Edition of the Tibetan Buddhist Canon* in 120 atlas-sized volumes. When completed in 1981, it was the largest collection of Buddhist texts ever assembled, and by some accounts the largest single publishing project in history. In the years since, Dharma Publishing and TNMC have been able to donate ten sets of the *Nyingma Edition* (currently made available to scholarly research institutions at a cost of more than $50,000 each). The list of recipients is as follows:

H. H. the Dalai Lama, Dharamsala

H. H. Penor Rinpoche, Bylakuppe

Sakya Gongma's monastery, India

Center of Buddhist Studies, Domkhar, Bhutan

Central Institute of Buddhist Studies, Ladakh

Central Institute of Higher Tibetan Studies, Sarnath

Ka-Nying Shedrup Ling, Nepal

Tarthang Monastery, Tibet (two sets)

Traling Monastery, Tibet

Two sets of the eight-volume *Research Catalogue/Bibliography* and eighty-four copies of the *Guide to the Nyingma Edition* have also been donated to Tibetan centers and lamas. TAP has participated in providing the funds for shipping these extensive collections abroad: a total of $134,124.

TNMC has also donated more than two hundred thousand thanka (sacred art) reproductions and more than a thousand copies of Dharma Publishing's books in English to monasteries and individual lamas, exclusive of books and thankas distributed at the Monlam Chenmo. TAP has participated in these gifts to a limited extent. For a list of all donations through 1996, see the tables on pages 140–42.

With the founding of the Yeshe De Project in 1983, Rinpoche initiated a new round of preservation activity. In the decade that followed, the Yeshe De staff, working under Rinpoche's close supervision, focused on the acquisition and publication of the collected works of the Nyingma tradition, the writings of the great Nyingma masters, and the works of major masters of all schools. This collection came to be known as *Great Treasures of Ancient Teachings*. Still an active project, with new texts being added each year, *Great Treasures* now consists of nearly seven hundred volumes, each in the same format as the *Nyingma Edition of the Tibetan Buddhist Canon*.

SPECIAL EDITIONS AND SACRED ART

The World Peace Ceremonies presented Rinpoche with a fresh opportunity for preserving and passing on the key texts

PRESERVING PRECIOUS KNOWLEDGE

For the past four decades, Tibetan civilization in the land of its origin has been poised on the brink of total destruction. Today there are signs that the worst has passed. Some monasteries are reopening, and it is no longer dangerous to admit to being a practicing Buddhist. Yet these changes, even if they endure, may have come too late. Tibetan culture has been drained of its native vitality, and the spirit of the people is nearly broken. Whether the tradition of Dharma in Tibet will be fully transmitted to succeeding generations remains an open question.

For this reason, I am compelled to do what I can to preserve and pass on the Dharma as we Tibetans practiced it in our homeland. For more than twelve centuries, the masters of Tibet offered their students great works of philosophy and spiritual insight, superb guides to meditative realization, and profound insights into the nature of reality and the place of human beings in the cosmos. Those of us who remember Tibet as it once existed must work to preserve its treasures. Such knowledge cannot be allowed to disappear from the face of the earth.

Between 1989 and 2001, the Yeshe De Project has offered nearly half a million books as free gifts. After the teachings of the Lord Buddha, this may be the largest quantity of scriptures ever offered to the Sangha. With these essential study and practice materials, the new generation can receive a comprehensive training that allows the Dharma to be maintained as a living tradition.

Distribution of Dharma texts on such a vast scale would normally be the work of a big foundation or a government project. For our small organization to make it happen, we have had to make great sacrifices. But we believe it is well worth the effort. In the darkness of the Kaliyuga, when people are wandering far from enlightened paths that offer meaningful direction to human life, the treasures preserved in Tibet may offer much needed light.

Although I personally possess no special skill or power, my experience over the past four decades has taught me that a lack of skill or qualifications cannot be an excuse for inaction. I have the deep wish to act for the preservation of this knowledge, and that is enough.

Tarthang Tulku

of the Tibetan tradition and the teachings fundamental to the Nyingma school. With lamas and monks assembling by the thousands each year at Bodh Gaya, texts could be distributed to representatives of the many monasteries in attendance, to individual practitioners, and even in some cases to lay people. At first the focus was on printing and distributing essential texts in immediate danger of being lost, but soon the project expanded in scope. Rinpoche set out to make available all the traditional texts required to sustain a complete curriculum of study.

Providing these new books, which came to be known as Special Editions, presented a new challenge to the Yeshe De Project and Dharma Publishing. For *Great Treasures* and the *Nyingma Edition*, previously existing works had been collected, duplicated, and assembled into sets, but for the Special Editions, Rinpoche determined to print the books in the traditional Tibetan style. In essence, this meant creating the books anew. Yeshe De staff, as well as staff borrowed from Dharma Publishing, typed the selected texts into a computer, the first step toward printing them in an elegant Tibetan typeface developed by Rinpoche for this purpose.

The decision to typeset the Special Edition texts in Tibetan script added new layers of complexity. Volume Five of the *Annals of the Nyingma Lineage in America* describes the process required to make this possible:

Texts typeset in the Yeshe De font are subject to a rigorous series of checks for accuracy. Each text is input twice, by two trained individuals. The results are run through a correction program that checks the Tibetan spelling for accuracy and flags questionable inputting.

After processing of the text through several other computer-based checking procedures, both of the corrected files are run through a file-compare program that highlights any differences between them. These variants are reviewed and resolved by experienced staff, who compare the typeset versions with the original texts. As their expertise has increased, file-compare staff have become more confident of their ability to flag possible errors as part of this process. The resulting file is printed out and thoroughly proofread against the original. All questions are referred to Tarthang Tulku or other Tibetan scholars. . . . After all corrections have been made, the text is formatted in Tibetan folios with Tibetan margin titles and folio numbers and given a final check before being readied for printing.

When a typeset text has been fully formatted, line drawings are added to the final typeset copy. The completed typeset folios are imposed and plated using a pyrofax process and printed at Dharmacakra Press. The paper used for printing is much thinner than the paper in the Great Treasures *volumes, but it is a special acid-free paper that has great tensile strength. Although it is much more expensive than standard book-grade paper, the quality and durability it adds to the finished books are well worth the extra cost.*

The printed folios are collated and assembled into Tibetan-style loose-leaf volumes, edge-dyed, married with endpapers and covers, and wrapped in the traditional manner.

The creation of texts and art for the Special Editions proved to be one of the most challenging and time-consuming projects that the Nyingma organizations had ever undertaken. The bulk of the work fell to the staff of the Yeshe De Project, which took responsibility for preparing the texts for publication under Rinpoche's close supervision. Since Dharma Publishing editors joined in this process for many months each year, production of English-language books was significantly affected. At the same time, Dharma Press dedicated much of its printing capacity to creating hundreds of poster-size sacred images to be distributed along with the texts, portraying enlightened masters, deities, teachers, mandalas, and other images important for practice.

The staff of TAP was eager to participate in this historic project, which had such great potential to benefit the cause of preserving Tibetan culture. Certain that it would be able to raise funds for this purpose, TAP agreed to take responsibility for shipping the texts and thankas to India and to cover other costs associated with distribution. At first this responsibility was shared with TNMC, but with the size of the Special Editions project increasing year by year, TAP soon assumed the task of paying all shipping costs. Since 1995, funding the annual shipments to India and elsewhere in Asia has become one of TAP's major responsibilities.

New Orders of Magnitude

The project of distributing texts and thankas through the World Peace Ceremonies began on a modest scale. In 1988, before the first ceremonies, TAP spent over a thousand dollars shipping thankas directly to Tibetan monasteries in India and Nepal. In 1989, TNMC members carried a few hundred texts and thankas to Bodh Gaya to distribute during the first Monlam Ceremony, and TAP contributed $7,077 toward transportation expenses.

For the second Monlam Chenmo in January 1991, TAP shipped eighty-two boxes of texts by air at the cost of $11,200. TAP made travel arrangements for the book distribution committee and paid their expenses in India and Nepal, but the airfare was covered by TNMC. As a related project, TAP raised funds to pay transportation costs to the ceremonies for students at the Nyingma Institute of Nepal.

For the 1992 Ceremony, Rinpoche made plans to produce and ship texts and sacred art on a larger scale. In all, fourteen thousand texts and twenty-five thousand thanka reproductions were readied for shipment. With so large a shipment, different arrangements had to be made. The books and prints were loaded onto three twenty-foot shipping containers, which were transported by sea from Oakland to Singapore, then transferred to another ship bound for Calcutta. In Calcutta, the containers were loaded onto trucks for the five hundred kilometer journey to Bodh Gaya. TAP paid for shipping, insurance, and inland delivery, a total of $9,417.

Above: Unloading texts from the trucks that had made their way to Bodh Gaya from Dharma House in Berkeley. Below: Monks and lamas study the texts shipped through the efforts of the Yeshe De Project, Dharma Publishing, and TAP.

Tarthang Tulku attended the World Peace Ceremony six times. Here he distributes texts prepared in Berkeley. The lamas, monks, and nuns received the books with the deepest respect and joy. In Tibet, such treasures were rare indeed.

THE HIGHEST EDUCATION

The quest for knowledge as practiced for many centuries in the Tibetan Buddhist tradition engages the most fundamental questions of human existence. In this context, the purpose of monastic education is to free consciousness from greed, aggression, and confusion, and to activate the full potential of human knowledge in the material, psychological, and spiritual realms.

Preserved by the lineage of masters in a living form that gives reliable results, education in a monastic setting is sophisticated and rigorous. Knowledge is made available to the student in specific orderly stages that allow a body of knowledge to be synthesized from theory and direct experience. Study of both religious subjects and the arts and sciences is required, including history, language, mathematics, and medicine, ritual arts and crafts, and sacred music and dance. Extensive memorization and reading form an essential part of the curriculum.

Religious studies begin with preliminary practices to refine body, speech, and mind through concentration, meditation, mantra, and visualization. Five distinct stages are practiced. First comes taking refuge in the Buddha, Dharma, and Sangha, making a full-hearted commitment to the path of knowledge; second, developing Bodhicitta, the intention to obtain complete Enlightenment for the benefit of others as well as for oneself; third, the Vajrasattva initiation that purifies karma and removes obscurations; fourth, mandala offerings that dedicate the merit and wisdom generated by the practice of the ten paramitas to the benefit of others; and lastly, Guruyoga, which unites body, speech, and mind with the awakened energy of the Guru, transmitting a living realization.

The studies at most monasteries are organized into three major divisions. . . . The first division is the study and practice of Vinaya, the guidelines for behavior that aim to stabilize physical, mental, and

Above, and next two pages: In a 1999 Gesar, *Tarthang Tulku offered insight into the significance and value of the texts distributed at the World Peace Ceremonies.*

emotional well-being, so that the student becomes a living example of the Dharma. The second division is study and practice of Sutrayana: teachings that develop dedication to serving sentient beings and transmit the profound, self-transcending wisdom that supports this intention. The third division is study and practice of Mantrayana: teachings based on the developing and completion stages of visualization and the two accumulations of merit and wisdom. Together, these practices gradually transform ordinary consciousness into enlightened awareness. They conduct the student along the path of liberation to its completion, bringing the relative and the absolute into perfect harmony.

Each of the three major divisions of study contains vast topics whose meaning is set forth in hundreds of texts. For example, the Sutrayana includes five advanced topics treated by the Indian Mahapanditas in the Shastra (commentarial) tradition: Logic and Epistemology, Vinaya, Abhidharma, Madhyamaka, and Prajnaparamita.

Taken together, these five subjects offer a comprehensive foundation for realization. The starting point is logic and epistemology, which establish the valid means of knowledge and make it possible to understand distinctions between reality and illusion, truth and falsehood, from the perspective of different levels of human perception. Next, the discipline of the Vinaya provides the essential basis for bringing balance and refinement to body, speech, and mind, so that the knowledge acquired through study and meditative practice can be embodied in a harmonious way of life, and thus brought to fulfillment.

The next topic, Abhidharma, investigates both human consciousness and the cosmos, analyzing the structure and patterning of reality as it is perceived and as it functions in experience. The operation of emotionality and the reality of the self are carefully questioned, and the inner workings of the ego are studied through close observation and analysis. Bringing this analysis to completion means penetrating the self's manifestations of hatred, desire, pride, confusion, and fear. This requires the skillful means of the Madhyamaka, the Middle Way that transcends the conceptual extremes of nihilism and eternalism and frees the individual from the illusions of the separate self. Release from these illusions opens the doorway to Prajnaparamita, the perfection of wisdom that cuts through karmic obscurations and transcends all limitations. Its foundation is the growth of Bodhicitta, which connects the student to the lineage of the Awakened Ones. As the ten levels of the Bodhisattva path unfold, specific antidotes to emotional patterns become available at each stage, so that enlightened qualities can manifest by degrees. At last, the way is open to perfect freedom.

These five topics of the Sutrayana are essential for overcoming the confusion of samsara. They make it possible to follow in the footsteps of the Tathagata, whether one takes the way of the Mahayana or follows the teachings of the Theravada. Because they call for a complete transformation in one's way of being, these teachings can take aeons to perfect. Yet the Mantrayana shortens this path, creating the possibility of complete awakening in one lifetime, as manifested in the lives of masters like the Lotus-Born Guru and the Eighty-Four Siddhas.

Even in our era of increasing pressure and confusion, the purity and power of the Mantrayana remain undiminished, as evidenced by the achievements of recent masters such as Jigme Lingpa and Jamyang Khyentse Wangpo. The depth of their wisdom and accomplishments gives us confidence that the inner light of the Bodhisattva's understanding can be generated by anyone who follows the Path of Awakening.

As long as the fundamental questions of existence remain unsolved, the intensive system of higher education followed in Tibet will continue to have great value. Knowledge that is embodied in the hearts and minds of individuals generates self-confidence, dignity, generosity, and joy. It is directly available to benefit others in skillful ways, to remove suffering, to clarify confusion, and to inspire creativity.

The final result of this education is mastery of the most advanced science of existence. The experience of twenty-five hundred years has demonstrated that the wisdom of the Buddha nourishes the heart of human being, granting the deepest human desires for knowledge, freedom, and happiness, and bringing human destiny under our control. The modern world cannot afford to lose this awakened vision—this precious body of knowledge that could never be replicated.

In 1993, TAP again paid all costs related to shipping, a total of $17,260. Three containers were shipped in all. As a further gesture of support, TAP sponsored the printing of fifty thousand small images of Guru Padmasambhava to be distributed to lay people, and also made a symbolic donation of $108 toward thread for additional banners for the Bodh Gaya Monlam.

With such large shipments being sent each year, costs threatened to become unmanageable. Determined to cut expenses, a TAP representative working together with the Yeshe De Project negotiated a reduced rate from Mitsui Shipping, the Japanese steamship company hired to ship the containers of sacred texts and thankas from Oakland to Calcutta. This generosity on the part of the Mitsui company has saved TAP tens of thousands of dollars.

From time to time in the course of the past decade, TAP has also made contributions to text production itself. The most substantial was in 1997, when TAP contributed $40,000 for this purpose. Further details on TAP's expenditures in succeeding years can be found in the next chapter.

PEACE CEREMONY PUBLICATIONS

In the spring of 1993, Tarthang Tulku directed Dharma Publishing to prepare an account that would document the purpose and development of the World Peace Ceremony and convey the historic significance of this annual gathering. For Westerners, the descriptive text and the inclusion of relevant canonical materials offered an opportunity to understand more fully the background of the ceremonies, while the hundreds of full-color pictures gave some sense of what it was like to be able to participate in these truly monumental convocations.

The first volume in what became a series of commemorative volumes was more than 250 pages in length. Entitled *World Peace Ceremony, Bodh Gayā*, it was published in time to be shipped to Bodh Gaya and distributed at the 1994 Ceremony. In later years three additional volumes were produced: one more on the Bodh Gaya ceremony and two that dealt with the Monlams of all Four Schools. Printed on high-quality paper and in full-color, the books were very expensive to produce. TAP shared this expense with TNMC, contributing approximately ten thousand dollars for producing the first volume and another $10,400 toward later volumes. In return, Rinpoche dedicated the income from sales of the English-language volumes to TAP's programs and activities.

Taken together, the Peace Ceremony publications offer a wealth of information about the central Buddhist holy places, the importance of prayer and devotion, the value of religious symbols, and the history and development of the Tibetan traditions of Dharma study and practice. The publications also celebrate the achievements of Tibetan civilization and present the World Peace Ceremonies as positive models for cultural restoration: successful experiments in effective ways to preserve ancient knowledge as a living lineage.

Books and thankas, sent through TAP's support, are distributed to the participants of the Longchenpa Ceremony held in Sarnath, where the Buddha first taught the Dharma.

Beginning in 1996, the organizers of each new Monlam have published their own annual commemorative volumes. Starting in 1999, the Yeshe De Project began producing a new series of annual Monlam books, written in Tibetan by Rinpoche himself. Three volumes have been published to date and widely distributed to Tibetans at the ceremonies.

CHRONICLE OF THE WORLD PEACE CEREMONY IN BODH GAYA, 1989-2000

WORLD PEACE CEREMONY I BODH GAYA 1989

December 22, 1989–January 15, 1990

Participants Seven hundred Nyingma lamas, monks, and nuns; hundreds of lay people, including four representatives from TNMC.

Recitations 300,000 Manjushri Namasamgiti

Ceremony Offerings

800 Tibetan books

300,000 butter lamps; oil and servers for lamps for 30 days

100,000 candles

Butter and barley flour for tormas

120 monks' robes; food offerings and kataks

Gold, jewels for the image of Buddha in the Mahabodhi temple

Brocade canopies for two Buddhas, main Stupa temple

Brocade hangings for altar and temple

Expenses

Offerings and ceremony	$195,941
Offerings to head lamas and monasteries	17,144
Text production	25,249
Text shipping	5,099
Travel expenses for TNMC delegates	37,452
Total costs	$280,885

WORLD PEACE CEREMONY II BODH GAYA 1991

January 1991. Duration: ten days.

Participants 1,500 Nyingma lamas, monks, nuns; 1,000 lay people, including six TNMC representatives

Recitations Manjushri Namasamgiti, Bhadracharya Pranidhana Raja (both recited at all subsequent ceremonies)

Ceremony Offerings

1,760 Tibetan books

1,944 art prints

216,000 butter lamps

200,000 candles

1,008 incandescent lights

1,080 flower garlands

4,000+ sculptured tormas

4,000 sticks of incense

100,000 food offerings

Kataks (ceremonial scarves)

Pure gold paint for Buddha statue in Mahabodhi temple

Daily offering for 1,500 participants

Transportation for 1,500 monastics

Tea, food, tents

Expenses

Ceremony expenses	$76,805
Text production	104,500
Art prints (valued at $2 each)	3,888
Shipping	6,975
Travel expenses for TNMC delegates	12,000
Total costs	$204,168

WORLD PEACE CEREMONY III
BODH GAYA 1992

January 4–13, 1992

Participants 2,500 Nyingma lamas, monks, and nuns from more than a hundred centers in India, Nepal, Tibet, Bhutan, and Sikkim. More than 2,000 lay people, including thirteen TNMC representatives.

Ceremony Offerings

11,600 books
25,000 art prints

Expenses

Ceremony	$82,049
Ceremony offerings, misc.	11,265
Offerings to head lamas, monks, and nuns	33,156
Text production	200,321
Shipping	13,041
Art prints	50,000
Travel for TNMC delegates	30,007
Total expenses:	$411,417
Additional ceremonies for the Sakya, Gelug, and Kagyu traditions	49,772
Total costs	$461,189

WORLD PEACE CEREMONY IV
BODH GAYA 1993

January 11–22, 1993

Participants 6,000 Nyingma lamas, monks, and nuns, including 133 abbots and lineage holders; 2,500 lay people, including fourteen TNMC representatives from Berkeley, Odiyan, Japan, Brazil, and Holland

Offerings

8,000 books
12,100 art prints

Expenses

Offerings, living expenses, and transportation	$157,660
Gold leaf for statues and offerings for head lamas	20,125
Text production	95,001
Art prints	24,200
Shipping	23,096
Travel for TNMC delegates	58,809
Offerings to the needy	6,500
Additional ceremonies:	
Gelugpa monastery, Bodh Gaya	6,000
Theravadin monastery, Bodh Gaya	1,129
Total costs	$392,520

WORLD PEACE CEREMONY V
BODH GAYA 1994

January 12–23, 1994

Participants 4,500 Nyingma lamas, monks, and nuns, including nine high lamas, 146 khenpos; six thousand lay people, and a delegation of twenty-nine

TNMC representatives from Berkeley, Odiyan, Brazil, Germany, and Holland.

Organizer H.H. Penor Rinpoche

Offerings

2,000 books

28,230 art prints

9,000 prayer wheels

1,440 booklets for
Dharma Wheel Cutting Karma

1,514 *World Peace Ceremony* books

3,000 Tagdrol (texts to be worn)

100 prayer flags

Banners: 160 Buddhist flags; large ornamental hangings for the site of the ceremony; yolwas (fabric decorations); 32 punz banners; streamers

Expenses

Ceremony expenses	$92,909
Text production	50,200
Art prints	56,460
Prayer wheels	100,000
Dharma Wheel booklets	10,080
Tagdrol	2,000
World Peace Ceremony books	45,420
Prayer flags	775
Banners	5,302
Shipping	10,123
Travel for TNMC delegates	64,588
Total costs	$437,857

WORLD PEACE CEREMONY VI
BODH GAYA 1995

February 1–10, 1995

Participants 7,398 lamas, monks, and nuns from three hundred centers; thirty thousand lay people, including ten

TNMC representatives from several countries and thirty TAP pilgrims.

Organizer H.E. Zhechen Rabjam

Offerings

31,250 Tibetan books

15,995 sacred art prints

Expenses

Ceremony	$121,654
Books	100,377
Art prints	31,990
1,500 bookmarks	560
400 monastery booklets	495
1,000 *World Peace Ceremony* books (valued at cost)	6,162
500 Tagdrol	742
5,000 identification badges	2,420
Equipment	18,000
Shipping	21,277
Travel for TNMC delegates	58,260
Total costs	$361,937

WORLD PEACE CEREMONY VII
BODH GAYA 1996

January 20–29, 1996

Participants 5,927 Nyingma abbots, tulkus, lamas, monks, and nuns from over three hundred centers in India, Nepal, Sikkim, Bhutan, and Tibet; thousands of lay people, including twenty-two TNMC representatives from centers on three continents.

Organizer Lamas from Sikkim

Offerings

17,535 books

24,283 sacred art prints

10,000 Guru Rinpoche prints

10,504 Dharma Wheel Cutting Karma prayer wheel texts, rolled for insertion

Gold leaf

100,000 butter lamps

500 World Peace Ceremony 1995 books

Expenses

Ceremony	$140,479
Books	56,730
10,504 prayer wheel texts	12,256
Art prints (valued at $1 each)	24,283
Guru Rinpoche prints	5,200
Cloth framing	2,126
Gold-leaf offering	400
Butter lamps (50,000 donated to Bodh Gaya)	81,000
Shipping	12,018
Travel/food, TNMC delegates	53,575
Total costs	$388,067

WORLD PEACE CEREMONY VIII BODH GAYA 1997

January 10–19, 1997

Participants Seven thousand monks and nuns including 146 khenpos representing 256 monasteries; lay people

Organizer H.E. Dzogchen Rinpoche

Offerings

14,000 books prepared but not sent (rescheduled for shipment in 1998)

Expenses

Offerings to participants	$40,768
Last day offerings	32,611
Transportation	35,433
Total costs	108,812

WORLD PEACE CEREMONY IX BODH GAYA 1998

January 28–February 6, 1998

Participants More than six thousand lamas, monks, and nuns from three hundred centers; thousands of lay people, including seven TNMC representatives

Organizer H.H. Penor Rinpoche

Offerings

23,920 books

121,393 art prints

Butter lamps

Flowers

Food offerings

Expenses

Offerings to participants	$66,910
Butter lamps, flowers	11,012
Food offerings	16,602
Books	233,935
Art prints	121,393
Shipping	53,332
Theravadin monks	60
Total costs	$503,244

WORLD PEACE CEREMONY X BODH GAYA 1999

January 17–26, 1999

Participants 6,000+ lamas, monks, and nuns from three hundred centers; thousands of lay people, including 18 TNMC representatives and 15 TAP pilgrims.

Organizers H.E. Orgyan Thobgyal, H.E. Rigo Tulku, H.E. Khocchen Tulku

Offerings

82,208 books

152,461 art prints

Butter lamps

Food and flower offerings

Kataks

Expenses

Offerings to Participants	$85,762
Butter lamps	16,669
Food and flower offerings	703
Alms	1,468
Theravadin monks	461
Kataks	685
Books	327,831
Art prints	152,461
Shipping	98,737
Total costs	$683,877

World Peace Ceremony XI Bodh Gaya 2000

January 6–15, 2000

Participants More than six thousand lamas, monks, and nuns from over three hundred centers; thousands of lay people, including 20 TNMC representatives

Organizers H.E. Taklung Tsetrul and H.H. Penor Rinpoche

Offerings

166,000 books

98,398 art prints

10,000 prayer wheel texts

Expenses

Offerings to participants	$85,072
Butter lamps	23,255
Flowers and kataks	188
Theravadin monks	105
Offering to Temple Management Commitee	233
Travel and hotel	2,056
Administrative	291
Alms	1,602
Books	587,035
Art prints	98,398
Prayer wheels	8,708
Shipping	118,280
Total costs	$925,223

SUMMARY OF EXPENSES (TNMC AND TAP)

Bodh Gaya Ceremony	1989–2000	1,377,378
Longchenpa Ceremony	1995–2000	307,453
Books	1989–2001	2,044,867
Thankas	1989–2001	830,422
Prayer Wheels	1989–2000	126,624
Shipping	1989–2000	208,342
Staff Travel	1989–2000	352,095
Total		$5,247,181
Labor costs		4,500,000
(15 people for 12 years at $25,000 annually)		
TOTAL		$9,747,181

These totals do not include the costs of sponsoring Monlam ceremonies for the other traditions of Tibetan Buddhism, or in Bhutan, or the cost of funding the Bodh Gaya Trust. They also exclude over one million dollars in costs for acquiring the equipment and facilities for production on this scale.

A FUTURE RICH WITH POSSIBILITIES

When TAP emerged from several years of relative inactivity in 1988, thirty years had passed since the mass exodus of Tibetans from the Land of Snow. The situation for the exile community was a study in contrasts. The chaos of the early years had largely vanished. Every settlement had its monastery or retreat center, and thousands of Tibetans were training as monks and nuns. A small number of individuals and some communities were even enjoying a modest level of prosperity.

All these advances, however, could not make up for the changes that had torn the world of the refugees apart. In Tibet, the monastic institutions that served as guardians of the Tibetan heritage had operated within the context of firm and unshakeable lay support. But the monasteries in the exile communities existed in unsettled environments, where Tibetans lived side by side with people who followed an entirely different way of life. Many found themselves in urban centers where the pace of life and the emphasis on acquisition and consumption undermined the values at the root of a monastic way of life.

Bombarded with worldly stimuli, monks came under pressures utterly unknown in Tibet before the diaspora. At the same time, monastic institutions experienced ongoing financial pressures. The simple way of life in Tibet had made it easy for a few villages to support a monastery, but life in exile was far more complicated and costly.

As for the vital task of preservation, the passage of time made the need for action ever more urgent. Only a few of the masters fully trained in Tibet, who had guided the exiles so well, were still alive. Soon the future of Tibetan civilization and the knowledge it embodied would lie in the hands of a new generation. Despite their good intentions and years of discipline and training, lamas born or educated in exile had never known what it was like to live in a culture and land immersed in the teachings of the Buddha, where the value and power of the Dharma were self-evident. Their concerns were different, and their outlook was necessarily different as well.

In Tibet itself, the situation was not encouraging. Travelers and observers

Opposite: Volunteers at Dharma House prepare sacred texts for shipment to the World Peace Ceremonies in Bodh Gaya

*Amidst the hustle and bustle of Bodhnath, Nepal, Tibetan women follow
the time-honored practice of circumambulating a Stupa.*

during the late 1970s and throughout the 1980s reported that the practice of religion and study of the Tibetan heritage was tolerated in many parts of Tibet, but such relative openness could not be relied upon. In 1989 H.H. the Dalai Lama was awarded the Nobel Peace Prize, and the Chinese authorities in Tibet responded by sharply curtailing all forms of Tibetan cultural and religious expression, fearful of political unrest. According to reports by Amnesty International, the International Campaign for Tibet, and Human Rights Watch, Tibetan monks and nuns who dared to voice their aspirations for the Tibetan people and Tibetan culture faced imprisonment, torture, and even death. At the same time, accounts began to circulate of drastic environmental damage being done to the land: extensive logging, nuclear dumping, mismanaged agricultural projects, and the extermination of wildlife. The repopulation of Tibetan cities with Han Chinese was viewed by many observers as a long-range plan to breed Tibetan culture out of existence in its homeland. The Chinese insistence that instruction in the schools be in Chinese was an additional source of concern, for it suggested to observers that Tibetan was becoming a second-class language. If this trend continued, the next generation might not even be able to read the great works in which the accumulated knowledge of the Tibetan people had been set down.

EXPANDING TAP'S CAPACITIES

Seen in this light, Tarthang Tulku's initiatives in founding the World Peace Ceremony and producing and distributing Tibetan texts took on added importance. Gathered together in prayer, the Sanghas of the four schools could appreciate more clearly their potential for working together. And the texts and art they received at the annual Monlam Ceremonies gave them the resources they needed for advanced study.

Intent on supporting these activities and helping the Tibetans meet the challenges that confronted them, TAP developed its capacity for fundraising and for attracting volunteers. From 1988 to 1993 TAP built a strong donor base and reached out in new ways to support both Tibetan refugees and those living in their native land. Annual revenues grew from $12,428 in 1988 to $113,580 in 1993, an increase of almost a thousand percent. During the same years, the number of active donors expanded from 86 to 441, and the staff grew from one part-time staffer to two full-time and two part-time staff.

With so much fresh new energy and greater access to funds, TAP was able to increase its level of activity. In addition to offering support for the World Peace Ceremony, the Monlams of the four schools, and other traditional ceremonies held within all schools, TAP made direct contributions to monasteries for rebuilding and renovation, provided funds for the education of monks and nuns, offered humanitarian aid, and donated money to artistic and cultural projects and institutions.

SUCCESS WITH MAILINGS

TAP began 1994 with two full-time staff, two part-time directors, and three part-time regular volunteers. Its database of donors had expanded to approximately 1,800 names. At Rinpoche's suggestion, the staff now determined to focus its efforts on mailings. A large number of brochures prepared in earlier years were the first to go out. Ads were placed to recruit volunteers, and soon the TAP office was bustling with activity. Volunteers also helped by staffing fairs and book shows where TAP provided information about the Tibetans in exile, sold books, and invited interested visitors to participate in hands-on work that would benefit the Tibetan people.

During the first half of 1994, TAP began purchasing mailing lists and sending out brochures on a regular basis. By June, 104,000 pieces of mail had gone out, and by the end of the year another forty thousand pieces had been sent. New systems were put in place for sending acknowledgements and letters to donors, offering gifts, and preparing

Tibetan Aid Project

"Beyond the beliefs of any one religion, there is the truth of the human spirit.

Beyond the power of nations, there is the power of the human heart.

Beyond the ordinary mind, the power of wisdom, love, and healing energy are at work in the universe.

When we can find peace within our hearts, we contact these universal powers. This is our only hope."

--Tarthang Tulku, Founder Tibetan Aid Project

Marking 25 Years of Support for the Restoration of the Tibetan Culture and Aid to Tibetan Refugees

Tibetan Nyingma Relief Foundation

Tibetan Aid Project
2910 San Pablo Ave.
Berkeley, CA 94702

Phone: 1-800-33-TIBET
1-510-84-TIBET
e-mail: tap@dnai.com

Non-Profit Org.
US Postage
PAID
Berkeley, Calif.
Permit No. 352

ABC

Tibetan Aid Project

This is the Tibetan Aid Project.

Dedication

The Tibetan Aid Project is dedicated to encouraging the progress of the Tibetans living in Tibet and in exile. We take this time to remember the recent sacrifices and hardships which the Tibetan people have endured. Our efforts are offered to the Tibetan people and their friends in the west. May older Tibetans continue to draw inspiration from the rich beauty of the Tibetan civilization, and may young Tibetans learn to appreciate their heritage more deeply. May the precious knowledge traditions that have sustained the people of the Land of Snows endure and flourish in the future.

Tibetan Aid Project
Tibetan Nyingma Relief Foundation
2910 San Pablo Avenue, Berkeley, CA 94702
1-800-33-TIBET
Directors: Tarthang Tulku, Wangmo Gellek, Javier Rockwell,
Tsering Gellek and Pema Gellek.
Advisory Board: Arnaud Maitland, Bob Byrne, Padma Maitland,
James McNulty, Robert Dozor and Richard Kingsland.
We are on the Internet! E-mail us at tap@dnai.com,
and visit our website at http://www.nyingma.org.
The Tibetan Aid Project is associated with other organizations including
Dharma Publishing, Nyingma Institute, Yeshe De Project and Odiyan Center.
Credit: Photo of Chin Gompa & Mt. Kailas courtesy of
Jeffrey Alford/Asia Access: Toronto.

pledge reminders. Other areas where TAP began to operate in a more professional manner included the processing of donations, cultivation of large donors, shipping protocols for gifts, books, and prayer flags, sales and invoicing, and more efficient handling of bulk mail.

The new emphasis on direct mail had a dramatic effect. By the end of 1994, TAP's mailing list had almost tripled in size, to approximately 4,500 names. For the year, mailings generated over $300,000 in income.

In light of such positive results, TAP began to design a new brochure, intending to send as many as 500,000 pieces the following year. Rinpoche provided extensive input and contributed a personally written cover letter. However, an experiment with sending self-mailers early in 1995 failed to produce a good return, and plans were scaled back. In its 1995 Annual Campaign Letter, TAP adopted a more personal approach, addressing all five thousand pieces by hand and including handwritten notes. When this more personal presentation proved successful, TAP adopted it as standard practice. In later mailings, the staff made certain to acknowledge donors as special friends and partners vital to the success of TAP's mission. Such care and attention, combined with the value of TAP's programs and the results they produce, may help account for the high rate of repeat giving that has characterized TAP's donor base over the years.

Mailings continued to be the key element in TAP's fundraising from 1994 through 1998, when TAP again mailed nearly 200,000 pieces. The generous support of Alpha Phi Omega, a service fraternity whose volunteers helped prepare the mailings, made it possible to increase the size of mailings without overwhelming TAP's small staff. At other times, TAP drew on the assistance of the Cerebral Palsy Foundation, which was able to prepare mailings for TAP at a fraction of the cost of a commercial mailing house. Although the dramatic success of the 1994 mailing was never repeated, during these years TAP's database grew from 1,800 names to about ten thousand.

Gradually the strategy of relying on mailings from purchased lists grew less effective. With TAP steadily adding the names of new donors to its own list, income generated from that list began to overshadow the amounts received from names on lists maintained by other organizations. Starting in 1999, TAP cut back its mailings to about 50,000 pieces a year, anticipating that it would increase the number and size of mailings in future years, as the names found on the most productive lists turned over.

The funds required to carry out mailings that could increase TAP's donor base strained TAP's directive that no money from donations be used for operating expenses. Most non-profit organizations accepted such expenses as a normal cost of doing business, but at TAP, the shift in approach was carefully monitored to make sure that the focus remained on fulfilling TAP's mission. Rinpoche issued new guidelines, asking TAP to limit overhead expenses to ten percent of income and to hold fundraising costs to fifteen percent. Although these limits would be impossible for almost any other non-profit organization with a similar mission, TAP has worked hard to meet these goals, while at the same time steadily expanding the range of its financial commitments.

NEWSLETTERS AND GIFT CATALOGS

In May of 1994, TAP purchased a production-quality printer, making it possible for the first time to design and create fundraising materials and newsletters of near-professional caliber in-house. Later that year, TAP sent out its first Annual Campaign Letter, a mailer that could be produced at extremely low cost, in keeping with TAP's mandate to direct as much of its income as possible to its program services. Despite the mailing's homemade appearance—or perhaps because of it—the public responded generously.

A second, professionally printed mailing distributed late in 1994 became the model for a yearly "Holiday Letter" that has also consistently generated a positive result. Other mailings have taken the form of newsletters that keep donors and supporters abreast of new projects and initiatives, and TAP has begun to make use of e-mail newsletters as well. At times TAP has also sent out complimentary copies of *Gesar* magazine, giving donors the opportunity to see how TAP's projects fit into the larger picture of Nyingma activities.

In 1995, TAP created its first gift catalog. The two-page flyer let donors and supporters know that it was possible to obtain videos of the World Peace Ceremony, as well as books relating to the

Ceremonies and to the history and culture of Tibet. Encouraged by the positive response, TAP has continued to prepare and mail a gift catalog each year at the start of the Christmas shopping season.

SPECIAL EVENTS

An important part of TAP's mission is to encourage individuals to develop a personal interest in the importance of preserving Tibetan culture. Toward this end, TAP has initiated or participated in numerous special events that reach out to the larger community of supporters. In January 1996, TAP held a World Peace Day Celebration, connecting participants in Berkeley with the World Peace Ceremony in progress at Bodh Gaya. That summer TAP greeted more than 9,000 visitors at an Odiyan Open House organized by TNMC, providing information on TAP's activities and offering donors prayer flags, books, and art. That same summer, and again in 1997, TAP staff gave tours of a Sacred Art Exhibit organized by Dharma Publishing. Through the years, TAP has sponsored receptions and special showings of videos that portray the situation of the Tibetan people in exile and in Tibet and the work of the Yeshe De Project, as well as slide shows on the most recent World Peace Ceremonies.

Over the past five years, TAP has had good results hosting benefit dinners, a practice instituted in the 1970s. Several chefs have donated their services, often working in improvised quarters to turn out elegant vegetarian meals. Featuring good company, pleasant surroundings, gourmet food, and music, such events

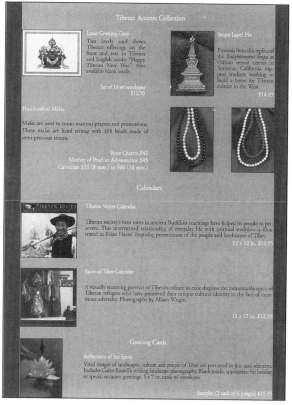

Excerpts from the 2000 Gift Catalog

offer an informal way to learn about what TAP does and how individuals can contribute to its programs. A dinner held at the Brazil Building in Tilden Park, located high in the hills above Berkeley, has become an annual event, with about a hundred people attending each year. Food and wine merchants have given generously in support of these activities.

The success of the Tilden Park dinners prompted TAP to organize smaller events in Marin and Sonoma counties and in Los Angeles. In 2001, TAP will take a further step, hosting an elegant dinner at San Francisco's City Club. Organized through the generosity of a leading San Francisco chef, this dinner will feature food prepared by seven internationally known master chefs.

GRANT WRITING

Over the years, TAP has made repeated efforts to obtain grants from foundations or other organizations that have a natural affinity for its projects. Several successes around 1990 (see Chapter Six) led TAP's staff to devote considerable energy to creating new proposals. When two applications in 1996 were unsuccessful, TAP sought the assistance of a professional consultant. In 1997 a grant-writing library was created and a form-proposal on behalf of both Yeshe De and TAP was prepared. Additional re-

With each new event, TAP has refined its presentation.

search was conducted, and in the fall of 1998, TAP's executive director participated in a grant-writing internship with Catholic Charities of the Archdioceses of San Francisco, which expressed its support by donating several books to the new library. As of this writing, however, these efforts have yet to result in any successful funding requests.

Encouraging Volunteers

By the mid-1990s, Dharma House, the space that TAP shared with Dharma Publishing and the Yeshe De Project, had become far too crowded to meet the expanded scope of operations. Midway through 1995, TAP joined in leas-

ing an adjoining warehouse. For the first time ever, TAP had its own office space. By 1996 TAP also had a website, located at www.nyingma.org.

The expansion of Dharma House offered new opportunities for attracting volunteers from the local community. Most volunteers came to help the Yeshe De Project with the production of Special Edition volumes going to Bodh Gaya, but others helped TAP with mailings, and those who came regularly sometimes took on greater responsibilties. In 1998, a volunteer created a TAP "Action Kit," a packet of information on ways to support TAP through writing articles for local papers, holding awareness-raising events, and participating in matching-grant programs offered by some employers. Designed to encourage friends and supporters to undertake projects on TAP's behalf, the Action Kit enabled individuals to work on their own initiative under the direction of more experienced members of TAP's staff. In 1999, One Day for Tibet, another initiative for involving the larger community, brought together seventy volunteers who helped prepare books for shipment to Bodh Gaya, finding sponsors for every book produced.

As TAP's range of fundraising and community activities expanded, regular donors began to express an interest in participating more actively in TAP's work. In 1999 TAP invited interested donors to join its newly formed Inner Circle, a group of advisers and supporters with a longstanding connection to TAP. The Inner Circle has helped TAP maintain continuity through a series of staff changes in recent years.

NEW PROJECTS

CREATING PRAYER WHEELS

After the expansion of Dharma House in 1995, TAP's friends and supporters found it easier to interact with the staff and participate personally in activities that TAP supports. An early example, which took place before the expansion, was a project in which TAP staff and volunteers helped create nine thousand handheld prayer wheels for distribution at the World Peace Ceremonies in 1994.

A traditional implement for religious practice in Tibet, prayer wheels enable

those who turn them to accumulate merit by releasing to all beings the blessings of the prayers and texts the wheels contain. In Volume Five of the *Annals of the Nyingma Lineage in America*, Rinpoche gives a brief account of prayer wheels and how they function:

Dharma wheels are vehicles for transmitting the blessings of the Buddhas. They are used to activate the power of sang ngag (mantra), zung ngag (dharani), and rig ngag (mantras compressed into single syllables), three traditional forms that encode the essential teachings into highly condensed expressions. All three forms of sacred speech are part of the lineage of transformation and are used in the practices of all Tibetan traditions.

Many centuries ago, the great master Nagarjuna learned how to combine mantric syllables to produce specific benefits. Investigating mantras like a scientist, he discovered that the blessings of these teachings could be released as effectively by turning them in prayer wheels as they could by recitation. The first Mani Chokor, or Dharma Wheel of Precious Gems, is attributed to this great master. Since that time, mantras and dharanis have been written on strips of paper and rolled into wheels turned by water, fire, earth, or air, or by the human hand, to release blessings that mitigate the force of karma and open the way to enlightenment for beings in lives to come. This heritage of knowledge for the effective combination and acti-

vation of mantras—has been transmitted in Tibet continuously.

In Tibet, texts prepared for prayer wheels are written in Tibetan script, a form of writing based on the Gupta script of India. Since the shapes of Tibetan syllables have never changed, Tibetan adheres closely to the original mantric syllables. The inner meanings of each shape and sound . . . have great significance, for each syllable is itself a symbol encoded with specific qualities of the Dharma. Arranged in precise patterns and set in motion, these symbols of enlightened speech release their healing energy to balance chaotic forces and bring peace and harmony to living beings.

Starting soon after his arrival in America in 1969, Rinpoche introduced his students to the purpose of prayer wheels. Within a few years he began to create the first large prayer wheels to be constructed in the Western world. This work has evolved steadily since then, as Rinpoche found ways to increase the prayer wheels' power and effectiveness. More than a thousand prayer wheels powered by electricity turn continuously at the Nyingma centers in America.

The prayer wheels that Rinpoche created for participants in the World Peace Ceremonies have been given the name Dharma Wheel Cutting Karma. Although small enough to be turned by hand, they made use of modern typesetting and printing technology, and were assembled in such a way that they held the equivalent of fifteen volumes of texts. In Tibet, giant prayer wheels known as mani dongkhor, or "ten-million mantra wheels," were highly venerated, and the Dharma Wheel Cutting Karma matched or exceeded their contents. Tibetan masters in exile were amazed that such a small wheel, measuring just five inches in diameter, could hold so many texts and mantras and enable a single individual to generate so much merit.

To create nine thousand of the Dharma Wheel Cutting Karma in time for the 1994 Ceremonies, TNMC students were joined at Dharma House by dozens of volunteers over the course of six months. TAP's staff took part in these efforts as fully as other commitments allowed. They also raised more than two thousand dollars to cover the cost of recruiting volunteers, reimbursing volunteer expenses, and shipping the prayer wheel handles from Nepal to Bodh Gaya. TNMC sponsored the production cost of the wheels themselves, a total of a hundred thousand dollars.

The prayer wheels were received at Bodh Gaya with overwhelming gratitude. In later years, TNMC and Yeshe De, together with volunteers at Dharma House, created and shipped many more sets of prayer-wheel texts, each printed and ready for inserting into traditional copper casings. Ten thousand prayer wheels were sent for the 1996 Ceremonies, nine thousand for the 2000 Ceremonies, and fifteen thousand for the Ceremonies in 2001. Many of these prayer wheels have gone to lay people, who rely on their blessings and power to forge a strong link to the Dharma.

Above: Monks and nuns with prayer wheels donated at the 1994 Monlam Chenmo. Below: The process of assembling prayer wheels must be done in accord with precise instructions.

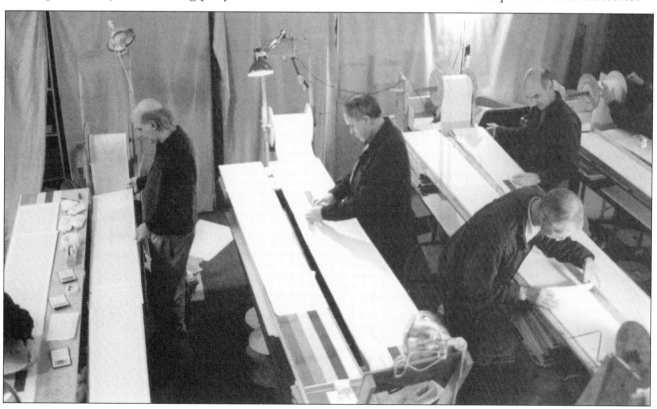

OFFERINGS OF PRAYER FLAGS

A traditional form of sacred art, prayer flags draw on the forces of nature to spread the blessings of the Dharma throughout the universe. Although few Westerners have the training to appreciate the symbolism of the flags, even casual onlookers are often moved by their beauty and inspired by the sight of their movement in the breeze, which can evoke feelings of deep calm.

The symbolism of prayer flags is based on complex arrangements of images and colors, which represent the Buddha families and the qualities they embody, together with their corresponding directions and elements. The chevrons attached to the flags continue this association with the Buddha families, for each is imprinted with the appropriate symbol and a mantric syllable in lantsa script. Chevrons on the right side of a flag direct its energy onto a worldly level; chevrons on the left side direct its energy to cosmic levels.

The prayer flag had its origin in the victory banners that honored royalty in India. It was thus natural for flags to be associated with the Buddha, known as the Jina or Victorious One, conqueror of illusion and negativity. In ancient Tibet, similar banners were commonly flown from the tents of warriors, so prayer flags were readily accepted as protective emblems. At temples, monasteries, and throughout the Tibetan landscape, prayers printed on pieces of cloth were fastened to poles, ropes, or trees, their bright colors signaling the presence and power of the Dharma.

One of the prayer flags authorized by Tarthang Tulku as a gift to donors

After Rinpoche came to the West, his students begin making prayer flags for the centers he established. In *Annals of the Nyingma Lineage in America*, Volume Five, he described this process:

Through the years, I have researched texts and questioned knowledgeable lamas in the process of introducing this tradition and expanding on its forms. Work on printing the Kanjur and Tanjur gave us access to the whole range of mantras and dharanis traditionally used for prayer flags. Selecting and combining these texts, I created large flags for specific purposes and locations.

After the texts are pasted up and proofread, an artist working under my direction prepares the artwork for review and correction. On final approval, the art and texts are combined and converted into film positives that are used for preparing silkscreens. The flags are printed on nylon sailcloth by TNMC students and sewn into flags with banded borders in contrasting colors. The chevrons are prepared in the five colors of the mandala. The background of the flags is usually yellow, gold, or orange and the borders are green or red. Substantial research has gone into locating the most weather-resistant and durable fabrics and strongest threads.

The time of printing is important: we often print flags when meritorious action is particularly beneficial; for instance, during a lunar or solar eclipse or other significant event. Empowerments are mixed with the inks as a special blessing. After the flags have been printed, sewing the chevrons and completing each flag takes even the fastest worker over an hour per flag; using fast industrial sewing machines, maximum productivity is eleven large flags in a twelve-hour period, while the average for an experienced worker is closer to five flags.

Over the years, flags have been prepared for protection and healing, for averting disasters, for the balance of nature, and for the vitality of the Dharma in the world.

In 1993, Tarthang Tulku gave TAP permission to print a set of Healing Prayer Flags and make them available to donors and friends who could be counted on to appreciate their sacred nature. Income generated in this way was to be dedicated to supporting reli-

gious ceremonies and the distribution of sacred texts. It could not be applied to operating expenses, or even to such worldly necessities as food, clothing or medicine for refugees.

The image area of the Healing Flags is 50" x 46" and their size with borders is 56" x 54". Each of the flags has the Ye Dharma Mantra across the top. The remainder of the flag contains homages and refuge prayers, as well as images, mantras, and prayers in support of the flag's central purpose. The prayers were chosen to counteract natural disasters, diseases such as AIDS, and other imbalances associated with modern times. There are seven flags in all:

Gesar Darchen: Good Wishes Flag for Success in all Actions. Images of King Gesar surrounded by the Four Guardian Kings. The Tashi Chogdrub and other blessing prayers are printed on either side of the central image.

Tenpa Gyepay Darchen: Light of Liberation Flag. Images of Padmasambhava surrounded by the Guardian Kings of the four directions, with the Tashi Chogdrub on either side of the central image and other texts and mantras.

Tashi Lhamo Gyedkyi Darchen: Goodness and Success in All Actions Flag. Images of eight dakinis, each holding one of the eight auspicious emblems, with the Tashi Gyedpa and other mantras and prayers calling on the Buddhas and Bodhisattvas to free beings from suffering.

Nyesray Gyedkyi Darchen: Eight Bodhisattvas Flag for Compassion and Wisdom. Images of the Eight Great

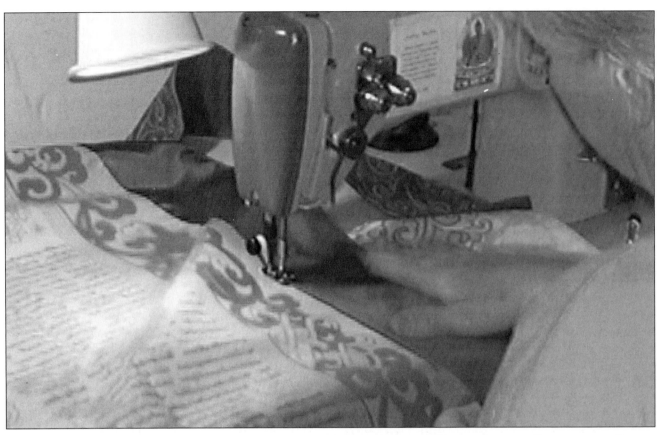

Above: a TAP volunteer at work sewing flags. Below: TAP staff at Odiyan silkscreening flags

Information on prayer flages distributed with each prayer flag that TAP offers its donors.

Bodhisattvas, with related mantras and prayers.

Sherab Nyingpo dang Dugkar Darchen: Flag for Transformation of All Obstacles. Images of protectors, including Ushnishavijaya in the center, Tara, and the great mother Prajnaparamita, with the text of the Prajnaparamita Heart Sutra, mantras, and prayers.

Tashi Chogdrub Darchen: Virtuous Compassion Flag. Images of the Buddha surrounded by Padmasambhava, Avalokiteshvara, Manjushri, and Vajrapani, with the text of the Tashi Chogdrub and other mantras and prayers.

Sherab Nyingpo Darchen: Prajnaparamita Wisdom Flag. Images of Padmasambhava in the center surrounded by Prajnaparamita and three other female deities. The central text is the Prajnaparamita Heart Sutra.

Initially the flags were made at the Nyingma Institute, but when Dharma House expanded in 1995, TAP took over the assembly and sewing of the flags, inviting volunteers to join in this special project. Soon TAP's overseas affiliates were participating as well.

The new project brought immediate benefits. Many TAP supporters welcomed the chance to have such potent symbols of blessings and realization flying at their own homes. The income from their donations was used to support the religious practices and studies of Tibetan refugees, completing a circle of auspicious blessings. These blessings were felt by many of the volunteers as well, who found that sewing the flags could evoke the quiet joy associated with meritorious action.

In 1996, Rinpoche encouraged TAP staff to become involved in the process of silkscreening the flags. In the spring of 1997, staff members went to Odiyan to help make five thousand prayer flags, fifteen hundred of which were made available for TAP donors. The project took a four-person crew two months. The following spring TAP staff again went to Odiyan to help with the flag-making process, creating another four thousand flags. In all, 1,800 of the flags printed during this two-year period were made available to TAP for sewing and distribution. Since it takes even highly experienced sewers two hours to sew a printed flag (beginners may take several days to complete a single flag), finishing eighteen hundred flags requires the equivalent of two people sewing full time for a year.

PILGRIMAGE

In 1995 and again in 1999, acting at Rinpoche's suggestion, TAP organized a pilgrimage to the four most holy places of Buddhism. The event gave some of TAP's close friends an opportunity to connect more deeply with the Tibetan people and their heritage. The focal event for both pilgrimages was a visit to Bodh Gaya to participate in the World Peace Ceremony. There (and again at Sarnath) the pilgrims were able to help with the distribution of texts and organization of the ceremonies. Traveling with experienced guides, the pilgrims also visited the three other major places of pilgrimage: Lumbini, birthplace of

the Buddha; Kushinagara, the site of the Buddha's parinirvana, and Sarnath, where the Buddha first made known the teachings of the Dharma. Thirty pilgrims took part in the first pilgrimage, and fifteen joined in the second.

The experience gained in 1995 led TAP to structure the 1999 pilgrimage along the lines of a retreat. Each day began with a one-hour group meditation, at which traditional prayers were chanted. Meals were generally taken together. Mornings were devoted to visiting pilgrimage sites, attending ceremonies (in Bodh Gaya and Sarnath), or working on projects related to book and thanka distribution or offerings.

Each evening throughout the course of the pilgrimage there were readings from traditional or contemporary texts. In Bodh Gaya readings from *Voice of the Buddha*, the life story of the Buddha, helped bring to life the significance of the Vajrasana, site of the Buddha's enlightenment. Readings from a text by Longchenpa on the meaning of taking refuge cast in sharp relief the opportunity that the Monlam Chenmo offered.

To prepare for their sunrise visit to Vulture Peak near Rajagriha, pilgrims memorized the Heart Sutra, spoken at that very place. Together they recited the text, then sat in silent meditation. In Kushinagara, where the Buddha passed away, a two-hour reading of the Mahaparinibbana Sutta encouraged pilgrims to reflect deeply on the significance of impermanence. In Sarnath, the pilgrims read of the life and teachings of Long-

Pilgrims in 1999 visit the ruins of Nalanda University, where great masters protected the Dharma and thirteen thousand monks studied the teachings of all schools.

chenpa, whose memory the ceremony there honored.

In Nepal, the pilgrims visited such holy sites as the Asura Caves at Parping and the Swayambhunath and Bodhnath stupas. They also visited Nagi Gompa Nunnery, Ka-Nying Monastery, and other active centers of Dharma practice. While at Ka-Nying, they had the good fortune to meet with Ven. Chokyi Nyima Rinpoche, a highly respected lama whose own studies as a young man were assisted by donations made through the TAP Pen Friend Program. Fluent in English, he spoke eloquently about the value of the work to which the pilgrims were contributing by helping restore to the Tibetan exile community the texts and art of the Tibetan tradition.

A NEW INITIATIVE: THE DHARMA TEXT INPUTTING PROJECT

At the end of 2000, TAP was honored to be asked by Tarthang Tulku to assume responsibility for a new program, the Dharma Text Inputting Project (DTIP). Its aim is to train monks and nuns to input texts in accord with the methods developed by the Yeshe De Project. The system relies on custom-designed software that makes possible a typographic flexibility and precision not available in any other system for generating printed Tibetan texts from typeset originals.

227

Monks at Taklung Tsetrul's monastery in Simla receive training in text inputting

While the Yeshe De Project has worked wonders in preparing more than one hundred volumes of texts for distribution to the Tibetan community, DTIP holds out the possibility of being able to do far more extensive work in the future. Equally important, by training Tibetan monks in the skills required to produce work to Yeshe De's exacting standards, DTIP looks ahead to the day when the Tibetan exile community will be able to take full responsibility for restoring their heritage for the sake of generations yet to come.

A generous donation from a TAP supporter enabled DTIP to begin oper-ations in December 2000. One of TAP's directors received intensive training in the methods used by the Yeshe De Project to assure accurate inputting, then traveled to Asia to train monks. Inputting projects were initiated at Ka-Nying Shedrup Ling Monastery and Nagi Gompa Nunnery in the Kath-mandu Valley; at Pangaon Caves in Manali, India; and at the monastery of H.E. Taklung Tsetrul in Simla, India. Although DTIP is still in the early stages of development, the enthusiasm of the participating monks and nuns has been encouraging.

CONCLUSION

As it enters its fourth decade, the Tibetan Aid Project has a base of thirteen thousand donors, of whom 5,500 are estimated to be currently active, giving at least once a year. Through the generosity of its donors, TAP regularly sends funds to more than twenty Tibetan monasteries and nunneries in exile and in Tibet. It also sponsors distribution costs for more than a hundred thousand Dharma books each year, together with even larger numbers of sacred art prints.

TAP supports the Monlam Chenmo Ceremonies of the four schools as well as numerous other ceremonies, and engages in a wide range of activities to help focus attention on the plight of the Tibetan people and the value of Tibetan civilization. All these activities support the vision of the Head Lama of TNMC, who continues to guide TAP in its activities and shape its mission.

The staff of TAP and all who are connected with its activities consider themselves deeply privileged to have this opportunity to help the Tibetan people preserve the heart of their civilization for the sake of all beings. In time, the world may come to better understand the value of the knowledge transmitted within the Tibetan tradition. If future generations are able to draw on this precious resource for the benefit of individuals and societies, then TAP's years of service will have been well-spent—an offering to the Dharma and to the whole of humanity.

TAP FINANCIAL DATA
1994-2000

INCOME AND EXPENSES

1994

Income	$367,234
Expenses	413,594
Net	46,360

1995

Income	$245,537
Expenses	220,230
Net	25,327

1996

Income	$344,173
Expense	295,000
Net	49,173

1997

Income	$312,163
Expense	294,903
Net	17,260

1998

Income	$344,389
Expense	355,300
Net	-10,911

1999

Income	$293,485
Expense	302,826
Net	-9,347

2000

Income	$228,987
Expenses	155,977
Balance	73,010

PROGRAM SERVICES

1994

Monastery support	$9,000
World Peace Ceremonies:	
Offerings to participants	40,000
Book distribution	5,393
Monlam book production	9,511
Ceremony photography	1,004
Storage and shipping of texts and thankas	33,927
Nyingma Institute Nepal	9,804
Shipping of prayer wheels	506
Refugee relief, laypeople	3,090
Monastery and retreat reconstruction in Tibet	50,794
Support for lamas at Odiyan	927
TOTAL	$185,158

1995

Monastery support	$12,533
World Peace Ceremonies:	
Offerings to participants	10,000
Book distribution	169
Invitations to 1996 ceremonies	350
10,000 prayer wheel kits (TAP's contribution only)	6,415

Monlam book production (TAP's contribution only)	2,070
Shipping of texts and thankas,	15,290
Shipping of texts and thankas for 1996	9,003
Storage of texts and thankas	21,200
Refugee relief, laypeople and independents	13,020
Monastery support, Tibet	15,000
Monastery support, Nepal	800
Support for lamas at Odiyan	2,700
TOTAL	$108,550

1996

Monastery support (total)	$76,975
Bhutan: support for six ancient retreat centers	18,000
World Peace Ceremonies: Offerings	40,000
Bodh Gaya book distribution Committee travel expenses	3,042
Shipping and book storage	25,200
Kagyu and Sakya Monlams	6,450
Support for individual lamas	2,125
Doctors without Borders, Assistance to Tibetan nomads	3,000
Gesar Dharma Troupe	4,000
Lama Serpo Building Fund (Bhutan)	2,000
Support for lamas at Odiyan	1,800
TOTAL	$182,592

1997

Monastery support	$300
Shipping of texts and thankas	78,563
Ceremonies:	
Five Gelugpa ceremonies	5,000
Tarig Tulku	10,000
Ka-Nying Shedrup Ling	3,000
Nagi Gompa	600
Pharping	6,000
Khocchen Tulku	3,000
Urgyen Tobgyal	3,000
Taklung Tsetrul	3,000
Sakya Trizin	3,000
Thrulzhig Dezhak	3,000
Tashi Jong Monastery	3,000
Nyingma Rewalsar	3,000
Rigo Tulku	3,000
Sakya Lamas College	1,000
Sang Ngak Chokhorling	600
Dzongsar Institute	1,000
Daddul Rabten Ling	600
Ngor Monastery	1,000
Nyima Zangpo	500
Khenpo Thubten Mewa	3,000
Zangdog Palri	1,500
Chogyi Trichen	1,000
Drikung Kyabgon Chetsang	1,000
Passang Dorji	1,920
Other monasteries	5,000
Odiyan Lama support	1,800
Kagyu and Sakya Monlams	10,327
Seva Foundation	50
Tibetan Meditation Center	40

TNMC	7,000
Assistance to individuals	1,896
Scholarships	5,000
TOTAL	$172,696

1998

Monastery and nunnery support:

Sakya Lamas Center	$3,000
Ngor Monastery	250
Taksang reconstruction	5,050
Pharping	4,500
Yeshi Lama	100
Chokyi Nyima	525
Shipping books and thankas	$98,737

Ceremonies:

Nyingma Monlam	$5,000
Sakya and Kagyu Monlams	10,000
Vajra Temple	216
Sakya School	2,750
Nyingma School	1,000
Gelugpa School	5,000
Kagyu School	5,500
Funds to Bhutan	5,000
Smaller monasteries	4,750
Chokyi Nyima	24,700
Nagi Gonpa	1,000
Chogye Trichen	250
Sakya Lamas College	250
Sakya Monlam 1999	10,000
Sakya Tharig	118
Namkhai Nyingpo	2,500
Trulshik Rinpoche	13,201
Lobsang Dorje	10,000
Odiyan	216

Assistance to individuals	1,193
TOTAL	$214,806

1999

Monastery support:

Men Tse Khang, India; Maratika Caves, Nepal	$5,000
Shipping books and thankas	$118,280

Ceremonies:

Offerings at Nyingma Monlam Chenmo	$2,293
Varna Longchen Monlam	15,000
Khenpo Thubten Mewa	10,500
Shaptrul Rinpoche	10,500
Khocchen Tulku	1,500
Rigo Tulku	1,500
Taklung Tsetrul	1,500
Urgyan Tobgyal	1,500
Sera Monastery	1,000
Gaden Monastery	1,000
Gyuto Monastery	6,000
Gyudmed Tantric College	7,000
Drepung Monastery	7,000
Rewalsar Retreat Center	1,500
Sakya Lamas College	1,000
Sakya Center	1,000
Dzongsar Institute	1,000
Ngor Monastery	1,000
Odiyan Projects	1,096
Assistance to individuals	1,045
Other	659
TOTAL	$197,873

2000

Monastery support:

Ka Nying Shedrup Ling (text storage)	$280
Shipping books and thankas (paid January 2001)	$77,960

Ceremonies:

Sakya Monlam Chenmo	$5,000
Kagyu Monlam Chenmo	6,000
Ka Nying Shedrup Ling	500
Nagi Gonpa	1,000
Taksang, Bhutan	1,000
Kurje Lhakhang, Bhutan	1,000
Senge Drak, Bhutan	1,000
Kyerchu, Bhutan	1,000
Sera Monastery	1,000
Drepung Monastery	1,000
Gyuto Monastery	1,000
Ganden Monastery	1,000
Gyudmed Tantric College	1,000
Shaptrul Rinpoche	2,380
Taklung Tsetrul	12,000
Dharma Text Inputting Project (paid Jan.–Feb 2001)	$21,527
Writing projects	$2,080
Special fund for upcoming projects	$50,202
Other	$431
Total	$188,360

TAP CEREMONY SUPPORT
1993-2000

NYINGMA

VENERABLE KHOCHEN TULKU
NYINGMAPA MAHABUDDHA VIHARA, CLEMENT TOWN, INDIA

9/8/94	Ceremonies	$500
7/1/95	Ceremonies	500
4/23/96	Vajrakila Sadhana	1,000
11/12/96	Tsog Puja	3,715
4/5/97	Lama, Yidam, and Dakini Tsog-bum	3,000
4/24/99	Ceremonies	1,500

VEN. MINDROLLING TRICHEN
NYINGMAPA MAHABUDDHA VIHARA, CLEMENT TOWN, INDIA

4/4/98	Amitayus Long Life	$300

VEN. LAMA TENZIN NAMGYAL
NYINGMA BUDDHIST MONASTERY, REWALSAR, INDIA

9/8/94	Ceremonies	$500
7/1/95	Ceremonies	500
4/22/96	Vajrakila Sadhana	1,000
4/5/97	Vajrakila Prayers, Guru Rinpoche Sadhanas, Tara Prayers	3,000
4/24/99	Ceremonies	1,500

VEN. RABJAM RINPOCHE
ZHECHEN MONASTERY, KATHMANDU, NEPAL

9/8/94	Ceremonies	$500

VEN. RIGO TULKU
NYINGMAPA MONASTERY, BIR, INDIA

9/8/94	Ceremonies	$500
7/1/95	Ceremonies	500
4/22/96	Vajrakila Sadhana	1,000
11/12/96	Tsog-bum: Lama, Yidam, and Dakini	3,715
4/5/97	Vajrakila Sadhanas	3,000
4/24/99	Ceremonies	1,500

Ven. Khenpo Rigzin Dorje

9/8/94	Ceremonies	$500
4/23/96	Vajrakila Sadhana, Tara Prayers, Barchad Lamsel	3,000

Ven. Rozar Gyatso

11/18/93	Kanjur Rinpoche Reading	$5,000

Ven. Shaptrul Rinpoche
Rigzin Drubje Ghatsal Monastery, Pharphing, Nepal

9/8/94	Ceremonies	$500
7/1/95	Ceremonies	500
4/23/96	Tsog,Vajrakila Mantras, Sampa Lhundrup, Barchad Lamsel	5,000
4/23/96	Barchad Lamsel, Sampa Lhundrup, Vajrakila, and Tara	1,000
9/16/96	Tarthang Tulku Longevity Ceremony, Amitayus Prayers	500
4/5/97	Lama, Yidam, and Dakini (10th, 25th), Tara Prayers	6,500
1/4/99	Ceremonies	4,000
3/1/00	Long Life Prayers	2,380

Ven. Taklung Tsetrul
Thupten Dorjidrak Aewam Chokgar Nyingma Monastery
Kasumpti, India

7/1/95	Ceremonies	$500
4/23/96	Vajrakila Sadhana, Guru Rinpoche Tsog	500
9/16/96	Tarthang Tulku Longevity Ceremony, Amitayus Prayers	500
11/12/96	Tsog-bum: Lama, Yidam, and Dakini	3,715
4/5/97	Phurba Tsog or Vajrakila	3,000
4/24/99	Ceremonies	1,500
7/25/00	Hundred Million Vajra Guru Mantras	12,000

Ven. Thrulzhig Dezhak Rinpoche, Kathmandu, Nepal

4/23/96	Vajrakila Mantras, 100,000 Taras, Sampa Lhundrup	$1,000
9/16/96	Tarthang Tulku Longevity Ceremony, Amitayus Prayers	500
4/5/97	Vajrakila Prayers	3,000
6/23/98	Hundred Million Vajra Guru Mantras	11,700
7/29/98	Vajrakila Sadhana or Guru Rinpoche Tsog-bum	1,500

Ven. Khenpo Thupten Mewa: Ngagyur Samten Chockhorling Institute, Manali, India

9/8/94	Ceremonies	$500
7/1/95	Ceremonies	500
4/22/96	Vajrakila Sadhana	1,000
9/16/96	Tarthang Tulku Longevity Ceremony, Amitayus Prayers	500
11/12/96	Lama, Yidam, and Dakini Tsog-bum	3,715
4/5/97	Lama, Yidam, and Dakini Tsog-bum	3,000
1/6/99	Hundred Million Vajra Guru Mantras	9,000

Ven. Urgyen Topgyal Rinpoche: Gyurmeling Monastery, Bir, India

7/1/95	Ceremonies	$500
4/22/96	Vajrakila Sadhana	1,000
9/16/96	Tarthang Tulku Longevity Ceremony, Amitayus Prayers	500
11/12/96	Tsog-bum: Lama, Yidam, and Dakini Tsog-bum	3,715
4/5/97	Lama Yidam and Dakini Tsok Bum	3,000
4/24/99	Ceremonies	1,500

Total Nyingma Donations 1993-2000 $125,955

KAGYU

Ven. Chokyi Nyima Rinpoche Ka-Nying Shedrup Ling, Kathmandu, Nepal

9/8/94	Ka-Nying: Ceremonies	$500
1/13/95	Nagi Gompa: prayers	490
5/12/95	Three Long Life Ceremonies for Tarthang Tulku	4,200
6/24/95	Additional Long Life Ceremony for Tarthang Tulku	715
8/19/95	Personal offering at Padma Ling	800
8/23/95	General support for monks	2,690
4/22/96	Ceremonies	6,300
4/23/96	Nagi Gompa: Tara Prayers	600
10/28/96	Kagyu/Sakya Monlams: Tsog-bum, 1997 Lumbini	6,450
4/5/97	Pharping: one year of biweekly pujas	6,000
4/5/97	Lama, Yidam, and Dakini Tsog-bum	3,000

4/5/97	Nagi Gompa: Tara Prayers	$600
6/12/97	Kagyu/Sakya Monlams, January 1998, Lumbini	10,000
12/12/97	Kagyu/Sakya Monlams, January 1998, Lumbini	10,000
4/13/98	Three-year offering for Daily Tea	24,700
4/22/98	Nagi Gompa: 100,000 Tara Prayers	1,000
5/18/98	Pharphing: 10th, 15th, 25th, 30th Tsog	4,500
7/29/98	Kagyu Monlam at Lumbini	10,000
9/4/98	Offerings at Nyingma Institute, Berkeley	525
2/22/00	Special ceremony for a lama's death	500
10/11/00	Kagyu Monlam at Lumbini	6,000
10/23/00	Nagi Gompa: Tara Prayers	1,000

VEN. DRIKUNG KYABGON
PHIYANG GONPA LADAKH, INDIA AND
JANG CHUBLING, DEHRA DUN, INDIA

| 4/16/97 | Tara Prayers or Tsog-chod | $1,000 |
| 4/4/98 | Kanjur Readings, Heart Sutra, Tara Prayers | 1,000 |

VEN. KHAMTRUL RINPOCHE
KHAMPAGAR MONASTERY, TASHI JONG, INDIA

4/22/96	Tara Prayers and Sampa Lhundup	$500
4/5/97	Lama, Yidam, and Dakini Tsog-bum	3,000
4/4/98	Guru Rinpoche Tsog-bum	3,000

VEN. URGYEN TULKU RINPOCHE

| 8/19/95 | Offering at Padma Ling | $500 |

TOTAL KAGYU DONATIONS 1993-2000 $109,570

SAKYA

VEN. CHOGYE TRICHEN, JAMCHEN LHAKHANG, KATHMANDU, NEPAL

10/11/94	Ceremonies	$500
4/16/97	Tara Prayers	1,000
4/22/98	Kanjur Reading, Tara, and Sherab Nyingpo	250

VEN. DZONGSAR GONGNA RINPOCHE

4/23/96	Prayers	$300

DZONGSAR INSTITUTE, BIR, INDIA

9/8/94	Ceremonies	500
7/1/95	Ceremonies	500
8/31/95	Ceremonies	500
4/23/96	Tara Prayers and Sampa Lhundrup	500
4/5/97	Tsog-chod	1,000
4/4/98	Kanjur Reading,Tsog-bum w/Tara, Vajrakila, Guru	1,750
4/24/99	Ceremonies	1,000

NGOR MONASTERY, MANDUWALA, INDIA

4/23/96	Tara Prayers and Sampa Lhundrup	$500
4/ 5/97	Kanjur Reading	1,000
5/13/98	Tara, Kanjur Reading, Heart Sutra	250
4/24/99	Ceremonies	1,000

SAKYA LAMAS COLLEGE, RAJPUR, INDIA

9/8/94	Ceremonies	$500
7/1/95	Ceremonies	500
4/23/96	Vajrakila Sadhana	1,000
4/5/97	Tsog-chod	1,000
4/22/98	Vajrakila Sadhana	250
4/24/99	Ceremonies	1,000

SAKYA MONASTERY

4/23/96	Vajrakila Sadhana	$1,000

VEN. SAKYA TRIZIN, SAKYA DOLMA PHODRANG, RAJPUR, INDIA

4/5/97	Vajrakilaya Tsog Pujas	$3,000
4/4/98	Vajrakila Sadhana	2,250
5/18/98	Sakya Monlams: Lumbini, 1999	10,000
4/24/99	Ceremonies	1,000
1/10/00	Sakya Monlams	5,000

Ven. Tharig Tulku (deceased)
Sakya Tharig Monastery, Kathmandu, Nepal

4/23/96	Stupa	$10,000
4/2/97	Stupa	10,000
6/3/98	Offerings for commemoration of Tharig Tulku's passing	108

Total Sakya Donations 1993-2000 $57,158

GELUG

Drepung Monastery
Mundgod, India

11/5/93	Ceremonies	$500
9/8/94	Ceremonies	500
7/1/95	Ceremonies	500
1/2/96	Tara/Sitatapatra Ceremonies	700
11/12/96	Kanjur/Tanjur Readings, White Tara, Heart Sutra, Sitatapatra	1,000
3/25/97	Kanjur Readings	1,000
4/4/98	Kanjur Reading, White Tara, Heart Sutra	1,000
4/24/99	Kanjur Readings	1,000
6/23/99	Special ceremony	6,000
4/10/00	Kanjur Readings	1,000

Gaden Mahayana University
Mundgod, India

11/5/93	Ceremonies	$500
9/8/94	Ceremonies	500
7/1/95	Ceremonies	500
1/2/96	Tara/Sitatapatra Ceremonies	700
11/12/96	Kanjur/Tanjur Reading, White Tara, Heart Sutra, Sitatapatra	1,000
3/25/97	Kanjur Readings	1,000
4/4/98	Kanjur Reading, White Tara, Heart Sutra	1,000
4/24/99	Kanjur Readings	1,000
4/10/00	Kanjur Readings	1,000

GYUMED TANTRIC UNIVERSITY
GURUPURA, INDIA

11/5/93	Ceremonies	$500
9/8/94	Ceremonies	500
7/1/95	Ceremonies	500
1/2/96	Tara/Sitatapatra Ceremonies	700
11/12/96	Kanjur Reading	1,000
3/25/97	Kanjur Readings	1,000
4/4/98	KanjurReading,White Tara, Heart Sutra	1,000
4/24/99	Kanjur Readings	1,000
6/23/99	Special Ceremony	6,000
4/10/00	Kanjur Readings	1,000

GYUTO TANTRIC UNIVERSITY
BOMDILA, INDIA

11/5/93	Ceremonies	$500
9/8/94	Ceremonies	500
7/1/95	Ceremonies	500
1/2/96	Tara/Sitatapatra Ceremonies	700
11/12/96	Kanjur/Tanjur Reading, White Tara, Heart Sutra, Sittapattri	1,000
3/25/97	Kanjur Readings	1,000
4/4/98	KanjurReading, Dugkar, Tara, Heart Sutra	1,000
4/24/99	Kanjur Readings	1,000
6/23/99	Special Ceremony	5,000
4/10/00	Kanjur Readings	1,000

SERA MAHAYANA MONASTIC UNIVERSITY
BYLAKUPPE, INDIA

11/5/93	Ceremonies	$500
9/8/94	Ceremonies	500
7/1/95	Ceremonies	500
1/2/96	Tara/Sitatapatra Ceremonies	700
11/12/96	Kanjur/Tanjur Reading, White Tara, Heart Sutra, Sittapattri	1,000
3/25/97	Sungbum Puja	1,000

4/4/98	Kanjur Reading, White Tara, Heart Sutra	1,000
4/24/99	Kanjur Readings	$1,000
4/10/00	Kanjur Readings	1,000

TOTAL GELUGPA DONATIONS 1993-2000 $53,000

BHUTAN

BUMTHANG THARPALING TEMPLE

11/5/93	Ceremonies	$500
9/6/96	Lama Mipham and Longchenpa Anniversary	500
11/18/96	Lama, Yidam, and Dakini Tsog-bum	3,000

JAMPA LHAKHANG

| 11/18/96 | Tsog-bum: Lama, Yidam, and Dakini | $3,000 |
| 4/4/98 | 10th, 15th, 25th, 30th Tara, Vajrakila, Guru Rinpoche Tsog | 500 |

KURJE LHAKHANG

11/18/96	Tsog-bum: Lama, Yidam, and Dakini	$3,000
4/4/98	10th, 15th, 25th, 30th Tara, Vajrakila, Guru Rinpoche Tsog	500
4/13/00	Tsog-bum Ceremonies	1,000

KYERCHU MONASTERY

| 4/13/00 | Tsog-bum Ceremonies | $1,000 |

VEN. NAMKHAI NYINGPO
LHODRAK KHARCHU MONASTERY

| 6/6/98 | Padmasambhava Pujas | $2,500 |

NYIMA LUNG MONASTERY

| 11/18/96 | Tsog-bum: Lama, Yidam, and Dakini | $3,000 |
| 4/4/98 | 10th, 15th, 25th, 30th Tara, Vajrakila, Guru Rinpoche Tsog | 500 |

Paro Monastery

11/18/96	Tsog-bum: Lama, Yidam, and Dakini	$3,000
4/ 4/98	10th, 15th, 25th, 30th Tara, Vajrakila, Guru Rinpoche Tsog	500

Pema Shedrup Choling

6/28/95	Ceremonies	$500

Queen Mother Kesung Choden Wangchuk, Thimphu

10/29/97	Ceremonies at Bhutanese Centers	$5,000
4/4/98	Prayers in the seven holy places of Longchenpa, with torma and tsog	2,500

Senge Dzong Monastery

11/18/96	Lama, Yidam, and Dakini Tsog-bum	$3,000
4/4/98	10th, 15th, 25th, 30th Tara, Vajrakila, Guru Rinpoche Tsogs	500
4/13/00	Tsog-bum Ceremonies	1,000

Taksang Monastery

4/13/00	Tsog-bum Ceremonies	$1,000

Total Bhutanese Donations 1993-2000   **$36,000**

BODH GAYA WORLD PEACE CEREMONIES

1/5/93	Offerings	$6,000
1/13/93	Offerings	1,913
10/7/93	50,000 recitations of Guru Rinpoche Prayer	456
10/21/93	Offering of fabric for thankas	378
1/10/95	Offerings	40,000
5/5/95	Butterlamp offerings	10,000
1/2/96	Offerings	40,000
1/12/98	Offerings	500
1/12/98	Butterlamp offerings	5,000
1/15/99	Offerings	2,296

Total Bodh Gaya Donations 1993-2000   **$106,544**

SPECIAL CEREMONIES

VEN. DUDDUL RABTEN LING
NYINGMAPA MONASTERY
MAHANDRAGADA, INDIA

4/23/96	Tara and Barchad Lamsel	$500
4/5/97	Lama, Yidam, and Dakini Tsog-bum	600
4/4/98	Vajrakila Tsog-bum	300

VEN. TAKLUNG NYIMA ZANGPO
OGYAN KUNZANG CHOKHORLING MONASTERY
DARJEELING, INDIA

9/30/95	Ceremonies	$500
4/5/97	Lama, Yidam, and Dakini Tsog-bum	500
4/4/98	Tsog-bum	500

PHUNTSO NYA YAB CHOLING MONASTERY

4/23/96	Vajrakila Sadhana	$1,000
4/4/98	Guru Rinpoche or Tsog-bum	500

SAMTEN DECCHEN CHOLING MONASTERY

9/16/96	Ceremonies	$300

SANG-NGAK CHOKHORLING MUDNDGOD, INDIA

4/5/97	Tara Prayers and Lama, Yidam, and Dakini Tsog-bum	$600
4/4/98	Tara Prayers and Lama Yidam, and Dakini Tsog-bum	600

VEN. ZANGDOK PALRI, NYIMA DRA-TSANG, DARJEELING, INDIA

7/1/95	Ceremonies	$500
4/5/97	Lama, Yidam, and Dakini Tsog-bum	1,500

LONGCHENPA CEREMONY (VARNA LONGCHEN), SARNATH, INDIA

1/1/99	Monlam Ceremony	$15,000

TOTAL SPECIAL/OTHER DONATIONS 1993-2000	$22,900

TOTAL TAP CEREMONY SUPPORT 1993-2000	**$511,126**

HOW TO HELP

TAP is able to offer its support to the Tibetan refugees through the generosity and support of its donors. Financial support is always deeply appreciated, but there are also other ways to offer assistance. These include volunteer work, helping to publicize TAP's goals and the situation of the Tibetan refugees, and organizing events or seeking support in your community.

At the donor's request, donations can be directed to any of the projects that TAP supports, from distribution of sacred texts to support for monasteries and nunneries or text-inputting.

If you would like to help, the staff of the Tibetan Aid Project would be glad to hear from you and offer suggestions. Friends in other countries can contact TAP's offices below. TAP also has representatives in Japan and the United Kingdom; please contact our main office for more information.

SUGGESTED DONATION LEVELS

Donor: $50   Supporter: $108   Sponsor: $500   Patron: $1,500

TIBETAN AID PROJECT
2910 San Pablo Avenue
Berkeley, CA 94702, USA
800-33-Tibet   510-848-4238
tap@nyingma.org   www.nyingma.org

Tibetan Aid Project
Instituto do Nyingma Rio
Rua Casuarina 297
CEP 22261-160 Lagao
Rio de Janeiro, Brasil
Phone: 21-527-9388
nyingma@barralink.com.br

Tibetan Aid Project
Nyingma Zentrum Deutschland
Wilhelmstrasse 28
D-48149 Münster
Germany
Phone: 251-296-247
nyingmad@aol.com

Tibetan Aid Project
Instituto Nyingma Brasil
Rua Cayowaa 2085, Sumare
CEP 01258-011
Sao Paulo
Brasil
Phone: 11-3864-4785

Tibetan Aid Project
Nyingma Centrum Nederland
Reguliersgracht 25
1017 LZ Amsterdam
The Netherlands
Phone: 20-620-5207
nyingmacentrum@nyingma.nl

FURTHER READING

BOOKS FROM DHARMA PUBLISHING

Ancient Tibet (1986)

From the Roof of the World: Refugees of Tibet (1992)

ADDITIONAL SOURCES

Adhe, Ama. *The Voice that Remembers.* Boston: Wisdom Publications, 1997

Bureau of H.H. the Dalai Lama. *Tibetans in Exile 1959–1969: A Report on Ten Years of Rehabilitation in India.* Dharmasala, 1969.

Dalai Lama, *My Land and My People.* New York: McGraw Hill, 1962.

Grunfeld, A. Tom. *The Making of Modern Tibet.* New York: M.E. Sharpe, 1987.

Karan, Pradyumna. *The Changing Face of Tibet: The Impact of Chinese Communist Ideology on the Landscape.* Lexington, KY: Univ. Press of Kentucky, 1976.

Richardson, Hugh. *Tibet and its History.* London: Oxford Univ. Press, 1962.

Shakya, Tsering. *The Dragon in the Land of Snows: A History of Modern Tibet since 1947.* New York: Penguin Compass, 2000.

Stein, R.A. *Tibetan Civilization.* Stanford, CA: Stanford Univ. Press, 1972.

von Fürer-Haimendorf, Christopher. *The Renaissance of Tibetan Civilization.* Oracle, AZ: Synergetic Press, 1990.

More information on the activities of the Tibetan Aid Project can be found in *Gesar Magazine* and in the five volumes of the *Annals of the Nyingma Lineage in America.* More information on the World Peace Ceremonies and on the traditions of the schools of Tibetan Buddhism is available in the *World Peace Ceremony Series* and the *Crystal Mirror Series,* both from Dharma Publishing.